H.E.L.P.

HOPE FOR EDUCATING LIFE-GIVING PEOPLE

WHERE DO I START?

A Guide to Help You Design and Build Your Homeschool Life

CHRIS & SHALA LATORRACA

THE HOME SCHOOL ARCHITECTS

*This book is dedicated to
our younger children, Saraia and Anthony.
Without you, we wouldn't be homeschooling parents.
You are blessings beyond measure in our lives.*

TABLE OF CONTENTS

INTRODUCTION

According to the National Household Education Surveys Program in 2012, there were an estimated one-point-eight million homeschooled students in the United States.

During COVID-19, Corey DeAngelis, Director of School Choice at Reason Foundation, conducted a survey of over 1,300 families via social media, and here is what he found:

- 23 percent of families whose children attended a traditional public school plan to send their children to a different type of school when the lockdowns are over.
- 15 percent of public-school families said they would homeschool.
- 16 percent of private-school students would homeschool.
- 13 percent of charter-school families would homeschool.

With that said, families who may have never considered homeschooling prior to COVID-19—when learning from home frantically became a thing—have now become open to the possibility and are researching this viable option for educating their children. Since you picked up this book, you may be one of those families.

But where do you even begin? We are here to guide you through the process of designing and building your homeschool life. We truly believe that you will love it! Our goal is to give you hope and help in your homeschool journey.

We have been homeschooling for nearly a decade. We didn't really have a clue as to what we were doing when we began—even several years into it. We do believe we have learned along the way and are continuing to learn. As we continue to homeschool and observe other families going along the same path, we've come to the realization there are certain things that apply to every family, yet every family's format will look different. Even if a family uses the identical curriculum as another, your family's personality, setup, location, and desires will come into play to shape your school day.

Our aspiration is to share foundational aspects that have worked for us and others with whom we have come in contact, as well as what hasn't been productive. We're super-excited to share our experiences with you and share some ideas that can help you as you take your first step. Remember, you do not have to have everything figured out before you begin. Take it one step at a time, one day at a time, and most importantly, enjoy—let me say that again, *enjoy*—the journey. It is a wonderful time to be with your kids and watch them learn.

The way this book is laid out is under the heading of "**Hope for Educating Life-giving People.**" Each letter of the word, H.E.L.P., will be a section of this book with chapters that support each topic. We tried to make it as simple as possible, so you can use it as a resource and go to the chapter you most need at the time. You will also notice we write as "we" and "our," but there are times when something relates only to one of us, and we will share whether it applies to Chris or Shala. And, at the end of each section, there is a place for you to make notes of what you want to remember.

We hope this is a timely resource for you and your family. Now, let's get started.

HOPE

"Desire accompanied by expectation of or belief in fulfillment."
(Merriam-Webster)

CHAPTER 1

YOU CAN DO IT

You may have fears that tell you to stop entertaining the idea of homeschooling, questions with which you are wrestling, and anxiety about what homeschooling looks like. That is normal. We are here to give you hope that you can do it! Remember, God put these little ones in your home for a reason, and you, as their parent, are the best one to know what they need. God created you to be the best educator for your children, even if you do not feel qualified. Let's dive in and help you with the practical steps to get you started on your homeschool journey.

DISCOVER YOUR REASON

In order to truly stay homeschooling for the long haul, it is very important to start with why you desire to homeschool. According to Simon Sinek, you need to "Start with Why"—we believe this applies to every area of life, including homeschooling. It is easy to homeschool on the days that are going well. But, as we have found, it is on the difficult days when you just want to throw your kids into a different school situation, until you remember your "reason." We go back to that "deep-inside-our-gut-knowing" that this is what we are called to do, in addition to more concrete items that we have settled in our minds. You, too, should evaluate why you want to move forward with homeschooling. It will help you on the days you feel discouraged. Here are some of the reasons for homeschooling that have been shared with us:

- Your child is having a bad experience in school and is being bullied.
- Your student is being pitted against their peers, and they're either ahead or behind them by educational standards.
- You just really want to homeschool your children.
- You are doing it for religious reasons.
- Your student has medical issues.
- You want a slower, less frantic pace of life, and thus, don't want to be hurried out the door every morning.
- You can focus on what your child loves.
- You can be your children's biggest cheerleader.
- You not only can work on academics, but also on life skills that you would like them to have before leaving home.
- You want to spend more time with your children.

Here are some specific reasons we have chosen to homeschool: first, Shala had a real desire to do so, even though it didn't really matter to Chris, at the time. Also, when we began, we were living in a school district we did not feel would be academically best for our children. As we have gone through the process, and are nearly ten years into homeschooling, we would also add to the list that our children are ahead of their peers in some subjects, and in others, are behind them. Homeschooling has allowed us to work at each child's pace. And we do enjoy that we are able to bring our religious beliefs into our homeschool setting and are not limited by what is allowed by the government.

Whatever your reasons, it is beneficial to determine what they are and write them down, so when you are frustrated and discouraged, you can go back to why you chose this path in the first place. For us, it didn't happen over night, but going back to the "reason" has kept us going; the dismal days are getting fewer, and we are having greater enjoyment as the kids are getting older.

After you determine if and why you want to homeschool, the next step is to do away with excuses. They may be valid explanations as to why it might be hard to homeschool; however, if you truly believe that homeschooling is the best option for you and your family, there are plenty of ways to make it happen.

Here are some of the comments we have heard mentioned, and maybe they will resonate with you—plus, we have created a hopeful way of looking at the opportunity of home education. We are sure that at least one of these "excuses" will capture what you are feeling right now:

Excuse #1: "I could never homeschool, because we need both of our incomes." Yes, it is easy to get caught up in the cycle of having two incomes and feeling the need to continue living at that financial level. However, a choice can be made to cut back in your outgoing finances, so you can live on one income. It may not be easy, but it can be done. We have found that having a home-based business in which we can both work has worked for us. We also eat at home, rather than eating out, and slashed the budget in any way possible. We know of other couples where the husband works outside the home and the wife has her own, home-based business, such as designing cakes for special occasions, or other opportunities. With remote working and learning, it is possible to both homeschool and work, given your individual circumstance. Be creative and think "outside the box."

Excuse #2: "I don't have the patience." Do you have patience with your kids all the time, right now? It is true it can be tiresome being both teacher and parent. Choose what is most important to you, what is necessary to fulfill no matter the cost, and what you should release, so not every push back from your child becomes a battle. This helps to simplify your mind and attitude.

Excuse #3: "But I'm not a teacher." Many homeschool experts have concluded that the best teacher for your children is you, because you know them and are passionate about what and how they are learning. You already are a teacher. You are your child's first teacher from the time he/she was born. You just might not have a college degree to display it.

Excuse #4: "I am a single parent." We recently touched base with a single mom of two, who has been homeschooling for about a year. One son is in second grade, and the other one is preschool age. After her divorce, the advice well-meaning people gave her was, "Put your kids in public school." She fought against this advice, because she felt she could do more for her children by educating them at home. She told us, "It has probably has taken me a whole year to really figure out what this needs to look like in order for me to work and make money and be a single mom and do everything—plus, teach my kids. I mean, you say it out loud, and it sounds a little bit crazy. But it all starts with a shift in your mindset about what education is."

Her encouragement to single parents is you don't have to recreate the wheel; use what is already out there, and don't be afraid to use some of the supplemental virtual learning academies. Also, use your evenings, weekends, mealtimes, and bedtimes as places to talk about historical events and such. She and her kids like to go outside after dinner and do a night sky journal. She concluded by saying, "When it's embedded throughout the day, it is a more natural approach to learning."

Excuses #5 and #6: "I think homeschooling is a great idea, but I wouldn't even know where to begin," and, "I couldn't afford the curriculum." For the issues of not knowing where to begin and also not being able to afford curriculum, we dive a little deeper into these in the next chapter, so if you will hang on for just a few pages, then we can help encourage you where to start and how to make this happen, so it can be affordable for your family.

Excuse #7: "What about my child's socialization?" We are so glad you asked, and this is a big concern. We hear it a lot from those wanting to homeschool, as well as from those who are afraid our children are missing out on friendships. We will be discussing this subject in depth in chapter 10, "Develop Relationships with People of All Ages and Stages." We will talk about what socialization really is and how homeschooling families and non-homeschooling families connect their children with friends in the same way.

Excuse #8: "What if my child has a gap in his/her education?" Guess what? Every child will have one. Every adult has one. We, as humans, cannot learn everything there is to learn about everything. However, we can instill in our children the enthusiasm it takes to become lifelong learners. If we succeed at that, then as they grow up, they can find the information and knowledge necessary for the direction they go in life.

Excuse #9: "I might screw up my children." This is a main thought in parenting, and something we can partially control, but ultimately, our children have to make their own choices. History has shown us many "screwed up" kids because of poverty, abuse, lack of education, and such, who have risen above their circumstances and achieved greatness. We can also see the opposite: those children who have received everything they need from their parents—or at least, so it seems—who end up squandering their lives. We must do our best and trust God with the rest.

Excuse #10: "I have a chronic illness and don't think I could make it work." Shala has rheumatoid arthritis, and it can be debilitating on some days. Yet, she knows you can make it work. She recently ran across an article by Sara Jordan Panning, from *Heart and Soul Homeschooling*, who has also had a chronic illness for over 20 years and has been homeschooling for over ten of those. Here is some of what she has to say: "Chronic illness can be unpredictable with no end in sight. Homeschooling, with its built-in flexibility, can be an excellent option for families coping with chronic illness." Some of her encouragement is to be flexible, read good books, slow down during a flare up, and give yourself grace.

Excuse #11: "I could never do that." And with that, we say a resounding, "Yes, you can! We know you can do it." Let us help cheer you on through this book. We believe it will equip you with how to make it happen.

DEVELOP CONFIDENCE

In addition to finding your reason to homeschool and doing away with the excuses as to why you can't, you need to take time to build your confidence. Believe you can move forward with homeschooling, even if you stumble along the way. It will take time to figure out exactly what and how you want it to look.

Here are some suggestions to get you started in this process. First, find others who believe in you and your ability to raise your kids in this way—friends, family, or another homeschooling parent. It helps to have external encouragement that can build you up. But, even more than that, you must have a deep-seated conviction for homeschooling. Stand on your "reason" that we talked about at the beginning of this chapter.

One more way to grow in certainty that you can do it is to read about others who are in the same situation. There are many books and blogs from which to pull information. One, in particular, is *SimpleHomeschool.net*. Written and compiled by Jamie C. Martin, she frequently shares stories from other homeschooling families and how they do life: she has a series entitled, "A Day in the Life." She has done a wonderful job, sharing stories of what other homeschooling situations look like. She shares stories from families with multiple children, all the way down to one child. Even if there are similar families, each family's home education will look different. It is encouraging to see what *can* happen and know you can create YOUR OWN look for your homeschooling situation. Remember, if they can do it, you can, too.

Thirdly, there are videos that teach us how to teach. One of our favorite YouTube channels from which to glean information is put out by Sonya Schafer of *Simply Charlotte Mason*. Her tidbits of information about how "to do" a certain subject are encouraging and are short, bite-size videos that can quickly be digested on a morning when we are feeling inadequate. She strictly follows the homeschool method of Charlotte Mason—of whom we will talk about in the next chapter—but just know, if you follow a different style, you can still glean from her, although not all the information will be as pertinent.

Finally, sometimes you must shut off the external voices and go with your gut, what your internal voice is saying. While there is good information out there, sometimes, we start reading and listening to so much information, we aren't able to truly step back and listen to that small voice inside of us that is telling us which way to go. So, while you read and listen to others on subjects, take time in the silence to find out what is best for you and your children.

Don't try to be perfect. There is no perfect public school, private school, or homeschool setup. There's no perfect family. There isn't a perfect individual. And there will be no perfect home-education style. You have to try to know your children, discover their learning styles, and go from there. Take it one step, one day, at a time.

We truly believe that this journey that you are embarking on is incredible. It is one of the most rewarding things you will ever do, yet it can come with some of the greatest challenges…ever!

We are here to let you know that YOU CAN DO IT! You might just need a shift in your mindset, and we are here to help.

CHAPTER 2

WHERE TO BEGIN

You may be wondering, "I thought chapter one was the beginning, so why are you saying we are just now beginning?" I guess we could backtrack and say that chapter one, yes, is one of the most crucial things for us as homeschool parents. If we do not have hope and know that we can homeschool, we will not proceed with it. But now, we want to start mapping out the "how." These will be practical steps that can benefit you prior to actually sitting down for formal lessons.

DETERMINE YOUR STATE (OR COUNTRY) HOMESCHOOL LAWS

Probably the most vital aspect of homeschooling, is finding out what the law says about homeschooling for you. For those living in the United States, you will want to find out what your state's homeschool laws are. If you live elsewhere in the world, you will want to research what is allowed in your country. Some areas of the United States don't require any notice, while others have low, medium, or high regulations. You will need to know in which kind of state you live and what they require. Items that may be needed might include: a certain number of days per year, specific subjects for certain grade levels, standardized testing at the end of each school year, or they will possibly require nothing at all. It all depends on where you live. So please, do your due diligence and seek out this information before you go any further.

Check to see what your state laws, statutes, and guidelines are. Laws, obviously, must be followed. However, make sure you know the difference between a law in your state and a guideline. We have found, in talking with attorneys and other homeschooling parents, many times the board of education and other officials will insist that something that is a guideline be followed, because their thinking is that it is actually a law. It may be unintentional, and they may not realize that certain areas are only suggestions, but we want to forewarn you.

For example, when parents withdraw their child from public school in Connecticut, the district may inform them they must complete a Notice of Intent. If you have done your research, you will know that the state *recommends* it, but it is not *required*; therefore, it is just a suggestion—much like a suggested retail price at the store. It is your choice, and you should research the benefits and negatives of following the guideline. It is crucial to understand what the law is in your state or country and abide by it. Know your rights. For those in the United States, here are three good places to begin: HLSDA.org/legal, NHELD.com, and HomeschoolFacts.com. These should be starting points, not an end all—and we aren't giving this information as legal advice. If you have questions or concerns, you should seek legal counsel.

DEFINE YOUR HOMESCHOOL METHOD

Although it isn't crucial to determine what method of homeschooling you would like to follow, it can be beneficial, so you can better choose a curriculum that fits your style. There are at least five agreed upon homeschool methods that exist: traditional, unschooling, classical, unit studies, and Charlotte Mason. Plus, there are others that are lesser known—like road schooling, world schooling, eclectic, Montessori, and

Waldorf—as well as any mixture thereof. I would just like to briefly touch on the five main methods.

Unschooling

This type of home-schooling environment is one that is student and interest-led. There is no set curriculum. Each day would be comprised of learning about what the student is interested in. For example, a student may be interested in knowing how Legos are made. On that day, you would do research and study about Legos and possibly use Legos to create a particular activity. On a different day, your student may be interested in finding out more about birds in your area, what their eggs look like, and how they grow up. You would spend the day studying that particular subject.

Unit Studies

Unit studies are centered around a particular theme. You would take one theme, or unit study, and revolve all of the other subjects around that. For example, your student might be studying weather. Writing, history, science, art, and any other subject that you have included in your homeschool day would revolve around that theme. You might even stay on that theme for a period of days, weeks, or months, depending on how you have laid out your workload.

Traditional

Of all of the homeschool styles, the traditional way of homeschooling is what most of us would have experienced in our schooling experience growing up; therefore, we are most familiar with it. It is textbook-driven and answer-based. For example, one would read part of the textbook and would then answer multiple choice, fill-in-the-blank, true or false, or essay questions. This might be the easiest to teach, because it is the one that most of us are familiar with. But it does not have to be the only option, and other methods should be considered—as we will discuss in chapter five, when we talk about your child's learning language.

Classical

The classical method of homeschooling is based on the Trivium–the three stages of teaching. The first is the grammar stage, which takes place in the elementary years. This stage lays the foundations of study, such as math, language arts, science, history, etc. It is about learning facts. The second is the logic, or dialectic, stage and takes place in late elementary to early middle school, when the student enters into critical and logical thinking. Courses might include algebra, debate, or other courses that help a student arrive at valid conclusions. And, the third is the rhetoric stage, which is focused during late middle school through the end of high school. This stage builds upon the other two, focusing on communication through essay writing, public speaking, and other specialized, rigorous course work.

Charlotte Mason

Charlotte Mason was an educator in the England in the 1800s who believed a child was a "born person." She did not believe that children are just blank slates when they are born—that God had already placed their personalities, talents, and preliminary skills within them. Parents would see those areas naturally develop as their children got older. Charlotte also held firmly that learning took place via three means: "the atmosphere of environment, the discipline of habit, and the presentation of living ideas." In other words: atmosphere, habits, and life. Miss Mason believed in children learning from "living books"—a book written by one author in narrative form about a single subject about which they are passionate and could be enjoyed by both adults and children—and literature.

She strongly encouraged the parents of her time to "spread a feast" of learning before their children. The feast would include, not only traditional academic studies—such as reading, writing, and arithmetic—but would also include art appreciation, music study, nature walks/study, as well as learning a foreign language, even in the younger grades. Lessons were to be kept short and focused, typically lasting during only the morning hours. The afternoons were a more relaxed time of learning—what we, as The Homeschool Architects, like to call "relaxed productivity"—which we will discuss more in chapter four. The Charlotte Mason method is the main one we have chosen to follow, but we have also bounced around a lot to get to this point.

Our encouragement to you is, determine the main homeschooling method you desire for your household. You may even decide to pick and choose based upon what you wish to achieve during a certain year, the subject matter you wish to study, or for any variety of reasons. The reason we think it is so important to try and determine your style from the start is so you do not chase after the latest fad or event. There is much good stuff out there, but as it has been said before, "Good is the enemy of great" (Jim Collins). It is so easy to get off track and follow what everyone else is doing, rather than what you sense is best for your homeschooling situation.

Find what is best for your family, and pursue that. Trying to do everything can and will lead to overwhelm and frustration. Know the main focus for your home education. Even write your vision down. Habakkuk 2:2 (The Message) says, "And then God answered: 'Write this. Write what you see. Write it out in big block letters so that it can be read on the run.'" There may be many days that you feel like you are in a frantic pace of life and having a clear, written direction can help you to refocus your homeschool day.

THE OVERWHELM OF CHOOSING A CURRICULUM

The reason we began talking about your homeschool method is because there is a vast array of curriculum available. Anywhere from choosing a boxed set of curricula, which has everything in it and is shipped directly to your front door, to picking and choosing each subject in your curriculum from various publishers. One can quickly become overwhelmed with what is available.

Our advice is to not begin by purchasing all of the homeschool curricula you can. You might not even want to begin by purchasing any curricula. You can begin schooling with just a bit of research about the subjects you wish to be part of the nucleus of your education—we share more of what the nucleus is in chapter five. There are both free resources, as well as those that you can purchase, which we share an extensive list of curriculum options in the appendix. Then, over time, begin adding in additional subjects. Take your time to build up your entire curriculum. And, as we have learned, there is no need to feel loyal to a specific curriculum, book, or subject material. If it isn't working for you, stop what you are doing and try something else. It is okay!

Since we are on the subject of curriculum, and because it can become costly, here are some ideas to cut down on the overall expense. First, you might want to look for free resources that are available online with the homeschool method you have chosen. You might choose to use a literature-based curriculum. For that, you might be able to find the books you need at your local library, or you might find good, secondhand copies from used booksellers, such as *ThriftBooks* and *Amazon*.

If you aren't using a free curriculum option, then here are some ideas. One thing we love is that some curricula can be used and enjoyed in one setting with all the children, such as history, geography, poetry, and foreign language. For those with more than one child, some studies need to be geared toward each individual child and his/her learning level, such as math and science. Keep in mind, if it is appropriate for an older child now, you can plan ahead for your younger child to use the same curriculum. Just go ahead purchase an extra workbook and test packet now in anticipation of that younger child using the same program; courses get rewritten periodically, and in a couple of years, the curriculum you purchased might be out of print—but the subject matter won't be out of date. For instance, we recently purchased a science curriculum for our soon-to-be seventh grader, and that will be needed in three years for our youngest child. We went ahead, because of the higher cost of this particular curriculum, and purchased the extra workbook and test sheets, so we would not have to spend that same large amount of money in three years when the curriculum might be slightly updated. This cut our cost in half, rather than doubling it.

An additional option for purchasing curricula is to buy used. There are several groups online, especially on *Facebook*, who might be selling just what you are looking for at a fraction of the cost. Also, many state homeschool organizations have used-curriculum sales at least once a year. In addition, when you are finished with a certain curriculum, you can then resell your curriculum and recoup some of your cost and put that toward the next year's studies.

By all appearances it seems that most parent educators are women. And while this may be the norm, it is very important to note that men play a vital role in the education process. Here is where we encourage you to begin discussing with your spouse—if you are married—what each of your roles will be. You may choose for one to be the sole breadwinner of the family, and the other to be the sole educator for the children. That's okay. It may be that both of you work in some capacity, yet one also does the majority of the teaching. You may decide to split the subjects in half between the two of you. It may be that one focuses more on life skills, and the other on academics. Whichever direction you decide to take, just be clear and communicate with each other who is responsible for what.

Up until recently, Shala has had the main responsibility for teaching our children. Our son, however, has had great challenges in math, and therefore, within the past year, Chris took over the primary teaching of that subject with him. Chris also brings life and occupational skills to the table, as well as a ton of historical knowledge. Both of us work, as we are self-employed in the same industry, and therefore, chores within the home are shared, as well. It has taken us over ten years to get to this point, yet we are doing better than ever with communicating what needs to be done and by whom.

Side note: Chris has found it very rewarding to be involved in the learning process. He has shared in the joy firsthand of seeing his children learn.

Since we started this chapter with where to begin, it makes sense that we conclude this chapter with keeping the end in mind. What do we mean by that? Know the outcome that you wish for your children, and we don't just mean graduation and getting a job. Our goal for our children is that they would become enthusiastic, lifelong learners. Know the character qualities you wish them to develop, the skillsets they will need before leaving home, and the type of knowledge you want them to instill in them. Begin adding those items in as part of their learning.

For example, we want our children to have more than academic knowledge; we want them to be well-versed in a variety of areas. In the section entitled, "Life-giving," we will be talking about going beyond what our children might be learning in a traditional school setting. Our desire is not for them to have tons of information upon completing 12th grade. Information can be found all around us, especially with the Internet at our fingertips. Knowledge in the truest sense is built within us by experience. We would rather have them know by experience.

CHAPTER 3

FIND YOUR SUPPORT TEAM

"Community is necessary! Without community, you make it harder on yourself, your marriage, your family," says best-selling author and speaker, Jackie Bledsoe. We, too, know firsthand how much human interaction is necessary–not just with our children, but with other adults, too. It is challenging on a day-to-day basis to connect with others, and during the COVID-19 crisis, it has given us a heightened sense of the need to be together, face-to-face, and not just via Zoom.

Let's face it. Life is hard enough as it is, but when the day-to-day interactions with people are taken away from us, as they have been during the pandemic of 2020, life feels like there's a void. As an extrovert who loves interacting with people, Chris has felt lost. As an introvert, Shala has needed more alone time, because there isn't a place for Chris and the kids to visit while she recharges. Not only do we feel more isolated than ever in our homeschooling, but other things have been taken away from us—no more hockey, baseball, or softball. No more watching our kids participate in other activities, nor spending time with our spouse outside of the home, and no more hanging out with friends at church. All of this was taken away and was been replaced with solitude at home.

All that to say, we need connection, and during COVID-19, we have seen this need magnified. So, in this chapter, we want to focus on a key component of home education—finding those who can support and encourage you, especially when you are struggling. Find cheerleaders along the way who can cheer you on when things are good and reassure you when things are difficult. We all need them during each stage of our lives!

START AT HOME

For those who are married, the first place you should look for support is your spouse. Our hope is from the get-go you both are on the same page with homeschooling; from there, you can be each other's first line of defense for encouragement. It is good to be able to lean upon each other during the home education process. We challenge you to be each other's biggest advocate and supporter, even if one does the bulk of the homeschooling.

We know, from experience, home education can put a strain on your marriage, because everything is being done at home, and maybe one parent feels like they're having to do "everything"—although, that may not be true; it may just be the perception. So, one aspect of being each other's support is to keep your relationship strong as a married couple. Here are some ways others have told us they do it.

One mom told us, "This is going to sound corny, but we email each other a lot. It's a way to keep a record of all the good things we want to talk about as soon as we get the chance. Then, when we get the kids settled, we'll check our inboxes and start chatting away. I guess it's just a way to say, 'I'm thinking about you and have something I want to share' until we can sit and connect that evening."

"We always exercise together, first thing," another mom said, "...great chance to catch up and chat. We make sure we have date nights most weeks and go away somewhere just the two of us. We also have separate friends for those times we just want to be us."

For us, we have coffee together every morning. We sometimes sit in silence during this time, sometimes we share funny stories, and many times, we talk about what we have going on that day or what we need to accomplish. We love to dream about the future, and we talk about the kids *a lot*. This gives us a time of connection before the day even begins and also helps us to know how to support each other throughout the day.

Alternatively, we work to encourage each other by understanding that although not everything we do—such as dishes or cleaning the house or yard work—is strictly homeschool-related, by Shala doing the brunt of the homeschooling, then Chris is willing and able to care for other aspects of the home which are difficult for her to incorporate into her daily routine. There has to be a give and take of what is being done in the home—the roles and responsibilities of tasks that need to take place on a daily, weekly, and monthly schedule.

For each family, supporting each other will look differently, but it boils down to communication. Opening up with each other about the hardships we face as home educators, how the other person can support you, and how you can support him/her. Talk it out, then walk it out.

YOUR INNER CIRCLE

Look for encouragement from among your family and friends. We understand there will probably be naysayers in that segment of people, so it will be best to know who to share with and in whom to not confide.

Find those who understand your reason for homeschooling and will encourage you to that end.

Find some friends, but they don't have to homeschool: they might just have similar values to you and your family. Ask them if they would be willing to come alongside you and allow you to reach out to them when you need it. It also may be that you haven't yet met the friends who will come alongside you on this journey. Those friends may come along as you move forward with getting involved in various groups. Also know that the first ones you reach out to may not end up being those who support you for a lifetime, but they may be the ones who open a door for you to connect with someone else who will be a long-term advocate for you.

Another part of your inner circle is your place of worship. Many times, you will find other homeschooling families there. The great thing about finding support there is you probably share religious reasons as to why you are homeschooling. We would encourage you to seek them out and begin connecting with them either via social media or by face-to-face encounters. We recently began attending a new church and are working to make connections there. In a random conversation with a staff member at the church, we mentioned we were writing a homeschool book and found out he and his family homeschool, as well. So, just a small interaction with a person can possibly turn someone into a part of your community.

EXTENDED ENCOUNTERS

In trying to build your support team, an avenue you will want to consider is finding those in the homeschool community. For example, you might look for a Facebook group near your geographic location. There are also Facebook groups based on your curriculum choice or religious preference. It is nice to connect online, because you are able to interact at your comfort level, as well as at a time that works best for you. Typically, you don't have to schedule a specific meet-up time, unless your group decides to do so. We connect with several Facebook groups, some that are local and some that are based elsewhere in the United States and even the world. In the age of technology, it is nice that we can have a community that extends beyond our specific location.

There are also homeschool conventions in nearly every state. These aren't necessarily a regular time of connection; however, they are a great, yearly time of meeting with other homeschooling families and gaining educational resources at the same time. There is usually a cost associated with them, and you will want to make sure that you block off that time on your calendar, but these can be a great time of meeting other families in your region.

Online webinars, face-to-face meet ups and playdates, and co-ops are also great options. Some of these can be found through Facebook groups, and for those in the United States, it may be through a homeschool organization in your state. Co-ops are a great resource. They do require a bit more from each family than just a meet up. Co-ops bring families together and draw on the expertise of the parents. Each parent is required to prepare for a lesson that is decided upon by them and based on the need of the group. Every family contributes, and every family is able to receive help from the other families, specifically in the area of academic studies.

Additionally, you can further your own education as a parent and take classes that would help you in leading your children. For example, one of the courses we work on is sign language. We learn from books and

DVDs; however, there are also sign language classes available for adults that we can attend to grow our skills, and then pass along the knowledge we have gained to our children.

If all else fails, and/or if you desire to do so, start a group of your own. We are sure you will find others who are in need, just as you are. A lot of times, it can feel like we are alone in our need; however, it seems that when we reach out to others, we find many are in the same situation that we find ourselves in.

ALL ABOUT YOU

And, finally, a big part of your own encouragement is YOU. In the Bible, David encouraged himself in the Lord (1 Samuel 30:6). He took the time, when everyone else was against him, and found his own source of strength. This may be giving the kids a little screen time, so you can rest or have a few minutes by yourself. It might be having your spouse, or a friend or family member, be in charge of the kids and getting out and enjoying an hour without being pulled upon every second. Basically, find some time to infuse life into yourself, so you can then pour that energy into the other humans with whom you interact.

You may not have a support team immediately upon starting homeschooling, but don't give up. If you remain diligent, you can develop it over time. Hopefully, though, you can find at least one person or group right away, so that you can have someone to lean upon when you are getting started. Or maybe, it isn't even a person you have actually met yet. We have been encouraged through podcasts, books, articles, YouTube videos, and other means. Many of our mentors don't even know we exist, but we are encouraged by them on a regular basis. Each of these groups of people can aid in helping you focus on what is necessary in the education process—not just on what you are feeling. You can glean ideas from them on what to do—or what not do—in a given situation, and they can assist in giving you a break from the day-in and day-out tension of balancing all you need to accomplish.

THINGS I WANT TO REMEMBER...

EDUCATING

"Education is the science of relations."
(Charlotte Mason)

Chapter 4: *Create an Atmosphere of Learning*

Chapter 5: *Begin Slowly*

Chapter 6: *Keep Going During Crises*

CREATE AN ATMOSPHERE OF LEARNING

If we're going to talk about creating an atmosphere of learning in our homes, it is probably important to define what an atmosphere is. We know that the term originally comes from two words in the Greek—"atmos" meaning "vapor" and "sphaira" meaning "sphere." Now, that doesn't translate exactly into our homes—a spherical object with gasses surrounding it. However, it reminds us that an atmosphere may not be able to be seen with our physical eyes, because you cannot see vapor or gas, but you definitely need it for survival—and you can feel or sense it.

We are sure that every one of us have been in a situation—not necessarily a school environment, but it could be work, home, school, or elsewhere—when you have been afraid and reduced to inaction because you were scared of how of someone would react to what you were doing. That is not an environment that is positive and uplifting, but feels like a judgment zone. Shala can recall going from a high-stress job into another workplace where there was grace and freedom to operate with her talents and skillset. She recalls feeling a sense of relief that the criticism and the overarching stress was gone. She was able to flourish in the work she was doing. That is the type of environment we want to develop for our kids.

Therefore, we need to develop an environment in our homes that is conducive to help them want to learn. So, how can that take place? Let's discuss that here.

Probably the first and most important aspect of creating an atmosphere of learning in our homes is the attitude we exude. We can provide a positive or stressful environment, a judgmental and critical situation, or one that allows for us to be ourselves and enjoy this time together as a family and as co-learners.

Philippians 4:8 from the New International Version of the Bible says, "Finally, brothers and sisters, whatever is true, whatever is noble, whatever is right, whatever is pure, whatever is lovely, whatever is admirable—if anything is excellent or praiseworthy—think about such things." Can we truly say that we are building a life-giving home in which we speak only things that are true, noble, right, pure, lovely, and admirable? Can we say that what is coming out of our mouths is excellent and praiseworthy? If we truly take this to heart, then, although we are not perfect, we can do our best to lay this foundation of affirmation in our homes and in educating our children.

If we exude a stressed, high anxiety, angry attitude, then, in spite of desiring a joyful, hope-filled, peaceful tone in our homes, our children will pick up on what we do and not on what we say. According to Leah at *My Little Robins*, "Creating a positive home atmosphere has more to do with who we are than what we do." We must change ourselves from the inside out for it to radiate throughout our homes.

One mother we connected with said she tries to affirm her youngest son by calling him CEO, which makes him feel important and built up. She also tells him how much she believes in him, and she tries to make sure she's attentive to him each day, taking the time to connect and get his thoughts and ideas. We, too, have found that if we give our youngest our undivided attention for 10 to 15 minutes, he is then able to work or play on his own afterward for quite some time. A little bit of positive speaking and attention goes a long way.

Jeannie Fulbright said, "If we make learning fun and about building a foundation for a love for learning, we will see our children succeed throughout their lives." If we create the right atmosphere, we can enjoy watching our children learn – not just now, but for a lifetime.

LEARNING = EXPERIENCE, NOT JUST ACADEMICS

Not only do we need to affirm our children, but we also need to provide an atmosphere for learning that goes beyond just academics. Shala recalls spending time in England back in the early 1990s, and one of her biggest takeaways from her experience there is that learning is not just head knowledge, but true learning is experiential—hands-on, interactive, and engaging—rather than just pumping information into our heads.

While we do need to help our children learn the academic basics, even that portion of learning can be interactive with our children, rather than having it be dry and boring. We need to create a way for them to look forward to learning the information, to make it a time they can enjoy and see little victories over time, even if it is not their strongest subject. Also, a great thing about home educating is we can provide lots of experiences for our children. For example, we know many families who study and experience nature as part of introducing their children to science. And for those children who are hands-on learners, it is nice to provide experiences for learning that are not strictly worksheet and reading-based, but engage their other senses, so they can better absorb the information.

Take some time right here and close your eyes. Either think back to when you were a kid or think about how your kids learned when they were younger—especially preschool age–learning was done through play. Play, obviously, is very hands-on and has been proven as one of the most effective ways for younger children to learn.

We found an interesting study done by the LEGO Foundation in November 2017. In their "Learning Through Play: a Review of the Evidence," they noted the difference between "surface learning" and "deeper learning." It is interesting to read what they consider surface learning is a lot of what seems to be an easier teaching style of lecture and listening. Deeper learning, though, tends to happen when there is a concept presented, then an experiment is done based upon that thought, and from there, the learner then can see what happens, and can finally reflect and comprehend what is true. Their firsthand knowledge helps them retain the information and put it into their remembrance. As Charlotte Mason said, "Education is the science of relations"—taking a concept and being able to connect it to a different thought in our minds is how we form links between information and retain the material better. Much like when we hear someone's name, we readily associate it to something in our mind that helps us remember that person the next time we come in contact with them.

Being involved, rather than being "taught at," is a more effective way to learn. A quote that has been attributed to Benjamin Franklin says, "Tell me, and I forget; teach me, and I may remember; involve me, and I learn."

Have you looked on Pinterest and Instagram and seen what looked like perfect homeschooling rooms? Yes, we have, too. They are beautiful, and we know that is what works for some families; however, for us, that is not what our lifestyle looks like. We also know that the great thing about home educating and setting up your "classroom" is it doesn't have to look like a traditional classroom. Home educating is not just doing school at home. This can be highly challenging, for some of us have grown up in the traditional school environment: it is the environment we have known, and therefore, it is seems the easiest to duplicate at home when we begin.

Some homeschooling parents have a dedicated space for schooling. We also know of others who do their educating at the dining room table, the couch, outside, while holding a chicken, while petting the dog, and any other variety of which you can probably think. Some families have larger homes that lend themselves to one style of setup, while others are in smaller, more limited spaces and get to be creative as to what that space looks like. Some have great bookshelves upon which to place their books, while others operate out of crates and boxes for their daily materials. Some even continue their homeschool journey while moving, which has challenges all of its own. This is one of the great things of home educating: being able to make our own space and the educating we do works for us, rather than it dictating how we should operate.

Kent Larson said in his book *12 Homeschool Myths Debunked: The Book for Skeptical Dads*, "Once I realized we didn't need to recreate the traditional classroom, and that we could customize our kids' education, I discovered a new type of freedom."

FREEDOM. Freedom to create an atmosphere conducive to learning. As we said in the first portion of this chapter, a joyful attitude is more pleasant and life-giving, rather than having all the correct stuff set up for your homeschool space.

A new thought for many parents, when creating an atmosphere conducive for learning, is to not schedule every waking moment for your children. First of all, this can lead to overwhelm and burn out for you, as the parent, because you feel like you have to be in charge and in control of every aspect of your children's day, since they are home with you. However, you should focus a small portion of your day on specific subjects you wish them to learn, and then allow for plenty of open time for them to learn through play—as we discussed earlier in this chapter— and other means. Allowing for times of boredom is where creativity is born. Children need plenty of time for imaginative play and constructive activities, or what we like to call "relaxed productivity."

For us, this time happens mostly in the afternoons when we may give slight directives, if they can't formulate a direction themselves, and then, we let the children continue from there. This time can include free time, but can also be interest-driven with items such as building, architecture, photography, craft items, indoor or outdoor activities, music, sports, recreation, volunteering, serving at an organization, building stilts, baking a cake, developing a spy organization—which is a current focus in our household—or anything that you and your children can comprise. Basically, the sky is the limit. The nice thing about this time, though, is you should not have to direct and control each step of the way. It may require you to plan in teaching some life skills or provide a ride somewhere, but it should not solely be centered around you and the direction you provide. While they are having their relaxed yet productive afternoons, Chris is usually working, and Shala is either taking some time to rest or working throughout the home on housework or our business.

As you can see, just as each person has his or her own personality, so each family has a way that works best for them. It can be nice to find out what works for other families; however, ultimately, it comes down to what works for you and your children. Don't try and duplicate traditional classrooms or what other families are doing; be open to what you see, but also be willing to set aside things that aren't the best for your home. You know what is best for you and your family. Trust that.

CHAPTER 5

BEGIN SLOWLY

We have found, in talking with parents who are considering homeschooling, that much of the overwhelm that seeps into their mind and emotions is from thinking they have to do everything from the very beginning. It is very important to remember that if you are deciding to homeschool for the long haul, or even in the short term, you have time to build one subject upon another. Our encouragement to you, who are new homeschooling families or are considering the possibility of homeschooling, is to begin slowly. Start off with just a small amount of what you would like to see your child learn, and then, as you all get a grasp on that segment of learning, you can gradually increase what you are teaching. Start small and build up. This is a time when you can grow together with your children.

BE A STUDENT OF YOUR CHILD

LEARNING LANGUAGES

We, as parents, have been studying our children since the day they were born. Watching how they respond to us when we tickle them, observing what they do when they fall down after taking a first step or two, and knowing if they have learned their ABCs. With that in mind, a new area we need to work on discovering is their learning language. Just as each of us have a specific verbal language used in the home and at work, so each person also has a dominant learning language. If we were to speak a language to you that you do not know, you will not be able to absorb the information we are giving to you. You might comprehend my nonverbal communication; however, what we are speaking to you will fall short.

There are anywhere from three to seven learning styles, depending on who you ask. The basic three are visual, auditory, and kinesthetic. We would also like to add in a fourth dominant learning language called reader/writer. As we've studied these learning styles, we have found that this learning style has elements that fit into the other types, but in reality, can be a stand-alone category, so that is how we will be treating it. We are aware that not everyone agrees with learning languages, nor the need to find out about them; however, we have chosen to study what has worked for us in our family and have found that understanding how our children learn is foundational to how receptive each one is to what we are trying to communicate. To us, it is no different than personality profile quizzes that are taken in the business world. It helps us understand each other, but it doesn't mean we put people into a box. It is just a starting point for communication.

Visual

Visual learners prefer to see what you are talking about. They prefer the use of pictures, diagrams, images, and illustrations to understand the concepts you are teaching. How do you know if your child is a visual learner? They might be a fast talker, be impatient, use verbal imagery, and need to see something when they have that epiphany moment.

Auditory

This language relies more on listening skills. Auditory learners, also known as aural learners, understand best when in the context of a lecture or group discussion. They may use verbal repetition to comprehend what is being taught. They may like to listen to recordings of subject matter and may gravitate toward audiobooks. How do you know if your child is an auditory learner? You might observe them as one who takes the time to listen and is slow to speak. They prefer to have you explain a concept to them, rather than reading the information in a book. They will listen and then be able to verbalize what you have said.

Kinesthetic

Kinesthetic, also known as physical learners, are those who learn by doing. They will use their hands, body, and sense of touch as part of their learning process. Additionally, they will learn through acting things out. These learners are ones who really enjoy lab work in science class or manipulatives in math. This type of learning can also be described as "hands-on." How do you know if your child is a physical learner? They may have trouble sitting still for a long period of time. They might be the slowest talkers of all learners, slow to make decisions, and may use all of their senses to participate in studying. They tend to acquire knowledge through trial and error, through problem solving, and through the hands-on approach.

Reader/Writer

This learning language, the reader/writer, could possibly be put under the visual learning style; however, we see the need to have it stand on its own. A person with this learning language prefers written text. They enjoy text-based input and output. Also, this style enjoys lists—bullet points and numbered paragraphs—titles, and headings that clearly explain what follows. They also like using dictionaries, glossaries, and thesauruses to find out the meaning and usage of words. How do you know if your child is a reader/writer learner and not just one who enjoys reading a good book? Some indicators for us with our daughter is that she devours books on specific subjects and can give you a detailed narrative, even weeks later, about the subject. She also has written multiple journals; one journal, in particular, is of her favorite vocabulary words and their meanings. She continues to search out the meaning of words and is intrigued when she inadvertently stumbles upon or intentionally finds new and interesting words. She is an avid reader and notetaker, and she is able to take something that is said or written and translate it into different words to help someone else understand what is being discussed.

LEARNING LANGUAGES WRAP-UP

Why is understanding your child's learning language important? You will be most successful in teaching them in their main learning language, which results in happier times for both student and teacher. The opposite is also true: you will find some of your most frustrating moments in attempting to instruct them with an approach that doesn't work for who they are.

We know that, as we have been homeschooling for nearly a decade, it is easy to fall into a rut of trying to teach each child the same. Shala is a kinesthetic learner. Our daughter is a reader/writer learner and is also very strong in visual and aural arenas. Even though they have different learning styles, she has been easier for us to teach, because this style was prevalent in the traditional classroom that most of us have attended.

Both Shala and our son share the same learning style, but the interesting thing to note is that she has a harder time teaching him, even though they each absorb information in much the same manner, because that goes against the way that was modeled for us in school. Re-learning how to teach curriculum is something with which we can relate.

You definitely don't have to have your children's learning styles all figured out to start schooling. In fact, just like us, it may take you several years to determine what their language is. That's okay. Just watch how they learn, and see if you begin to speak their language.

LEARNING READINESS

As you continue to study your children and learn how they best operate, it is important to know when to not push your children. They may not be ready to learn a certain subject yet. One of our children has had difficulty with math, and the other has had challenges with learning to read. It would be easy to continue to push them, but it would be exhausting for both student and parent.

Learn to back off, if necessary, and add things back in over time. We have taken steps back with both children. At one point, we completely stopped math for our older child until we could locate something that was on her level and geared toward her learning language. It is still a challenge, so we keep modifying what that looks like—but we slowly move forward with her. Our youngest child had a reluctance to reading and found decoding the words challenging; we backed off, and then, began to add in a simplified reading program that would have been well below his grade level in other educational arenas. The great thing with homeschooling is we can go at each child's pace, so they can feel victorious when they overcome the challenges they are having in a specific subject, rather than feeling like a failure because they are behind their peers.

As you begin walking down the path of formal academics, we would encourage you not to attempt teaching every subject you think your child needs. We have discovered that as we scale back to what we call the "nucleus" of our curriculum, this group of courses will be different for each family.

What do I mean by the nucleus? In science, the nucleus is defined as "the central and most important part of an object, movement, or group; forming the basis for its activity and growth" (Oxford Languages). So, while others may call it the core or foundation curriculum, our word choice is the "nucleus." This group of subjects is around which all other studies revolve.

Our view of each day is if all we do the nucleus of our curriculum, then we have succeeded in formal academic learning. Our nucleus includes Bible scripture memory, history, and geography. Anything else we are able to complete that day, or week, just adds to the learning process and is what they call "icing on the cake." Your nucleus will probably be different. It should be comprised of only two to four subjects that are the most important to you for your children.

KEEP LESSONS SHORT AND FOCUSED

During the COVID-19 crisis, when children had to begin learning at home with parental oversight in conjunction with their schools, there was a misconception that one has to be in school from nine in the morning to three in the afternoon. That may be how it's been done in both public and private schools, but there are varying circumstances which cause the school day to be that lengthy. One must take into account that there are a higher number of students in each classroom than would be found in the home, and there is transition time from classroom to classroom or subject to subject, plus regular school includes times for lunch and maybe recess. Because of these variances, the school day is much longer than it needs to be when one is home educating.

The beauty of homeschooling is you have a smaller number of students under your care, which allows you to reduce the amount of time spent in academic learning. Because of this setup, the amount of time per academic course is drastically reduced from other learning environments. As discussed earlier, begin with your "nucleus." For us, our nucleus takes anywhere from 30 to 45 minutes. Is that doable? We think everyone would say a resounding, "YES!"

As you proceed with that—even for a few weeks, if necessary—then begin adding in further subjects slowly—and we do mean *slowly*. Since we have two students with whom we are working, we would then increase our "work together" subjects. We do the nucleus collectively, and then, might add in the following: a family read-aloud (20 minutes), a poetry reading (5 minutes), a music composer study (10 minutes), and nature study (15 to 30 minutes). As you can see, we are now only up to a little less than two hours, and we have a variety of enjoyable subjects. For our soon-to-be fourth grader, we will eventually add in specific courses for him that add an extra hour; and for our soon-to-be seventh grader, she will have individual studies totaling one-and-a-half hours. Thus, beginning at nine a.m. and going to about twelve or one p.m. is a very doable scenario. Because you can help your student be intensely focused and bring his or her best effort into each subject, the time it takes to cover the material in a given subject should be anywhere from five to thirty minutes. Keep your lessons short. And, as I've mentioned before, if all you complete that day is the nucleus, you have a victory to be celebrated!

We hope this gives you encouragement on your journey. You don't have to keep up with what everyone else is doing. You can go at the pace that is necessary for you and your family. In the upcoming chapter, we will discuss how to keep going in the midst of crises, which can appear at first glance to be a huge roadblock to our children's education. So, stick around!

CHAPTER 6

KEEP GOING DURING CRISES 

We have lived through crises—not just the COVID-19 pandemic—but life has not been easy since we got married, over ten years ago. From Shala having mononucleosis on our wedding day, to starting our own business at the same time that we found out she was pregnant, to a job loss, to starting homeschooling, to moving homes multiple times, to becoming therapeutic foster parents, to caring for a loved one with dementia, to Shala being diagnosed with a chronic illness, life has been anything but easy, and we are no strangers to challenges. We have been derailed, sidelined, and paused in homeschooling for brief periods of time; however, we have kept going, and we know that if and when a crisis hits your family, you can keep moving forward, too! In this chapter, we hope to give you some ideas to help you think through how to keep homeschooling when it feels like it would be easier to throw in the towel.

Here is the advice from a homeschooling mom with whom we spoke, "Having homeschooled through years of various trauma, what I've learned: to drop the demand we place on ourselves and our kids. Life is more than academics. You don't have to keep up with anyone. You have permission to be. Breathe. Hold your babies. Laugh together as much as you can. Get small again. Explore life together with them in the micro, by becoming aware of and grateful for even the smallest things. Gratefulness is soothing, healing. If you're worried about academics, then read. Read and read and read. The rest will follow. Life will get better, and you will heal faster and be ready for the next season if you love yourself through this one."

Our very first suggestion is to pause and take a deep breath. We heard from many families when the COVID-19 pandemic hit, and everyone began schooling from home. Parents quickly became overwhelmed and couldn't fathom how to juggle work and remote learning. Overnight, their children went from going to a school building to home now becoming the place of education with parents becoming the primary overseers. They had no idea where to start, and many were losing sleep over their children's education. Some quit, while others tried to muddle through. The consensus was if they didn't keep going, their children were going to lose traction in their education.

We have heard from veteran homeschooling families about how taking some time off to evaluate, to breathe, and to refocus on what is important for the education process hasn't hindered their children's learning as long as it does not go on for an extended period of time. Taking some time off can help reset your kids' focus and energy, as well as can give you a break and can help you relax as you restart the process of educating your children from home.

During this time of pause, you can do simple educational things if you want. Find some educational shows, point your kids in the direction of imaginative play, take a relaxing nature walk and enjoy the beauty outside, play some board games that have an educational twist, or just give your kids and yourself the time off. It's okay to take a break from intentionally schooling. That's the beauty of home educating and being in charge of your child's education. We, as parents, know what is best for them and us, and we can move forward with that in mind.

After you pause, breathe, and evaluate where you and your family are in the crisis, then you can develop what plan of action should be put into place. Our suggestion is to scale back and start small. As we talked about in chapter five, look at what your "nucleus" is, and begin there. Don't try to continue doing everything in the midst of crises. You will become overwhelmed and frustrated, and more than likely, you will feel like quitting.

This is also a good time to go back to what we talked about in chapter one about discovering your "reason" for homeschooling. It is in these dark times that we have to go back to the very fundamentals and remember why we believe strongly in educating our children at home.

A great reminder is that you are not going to screw up your children, even if you do not homeschool for a time. It is amazing how God created them to learn via other means than just in a classroom setting. We remember being in a state of transition, living in a hotel after our house sold, and several homes we were trying to purchase kept falling through. During this time, our son, who was probably kindergarten age, began learning how to make the letters in the alphabet using Lego pieces. It was definitely not instigated by us, but it was out of his imagination and creativity that he was learning on his own. Our daughter has used times of crises to engross herself even more into books. She has read multiple books and learned so many facts from just her desire to read. If we allow our children flexibility and opportunities to learn, they can continue educating themselves, even if we are not the primary teachers.

A friend of ours tells of the time when her father was in the hospital. During this time, she was homeschooling her daughter—now an adult— and they had to decide how to homeschool through this time. She would pack up her supplies and would take them along with them to the hospital. While they were sitting with her father, she would also homeschool her daughter. Another way they would do "portable" schooling is through life skills, which we will discuss in greater length in chapter eight. That would be things such as going to the grocery store and buying three pounds of bananas at $0.33 a pound and asking how much that would cost. Doing simple things while visiting places of necessity can be turned into learning experiences.

It might not even be making it portable outside of the home, but for those with a chronic illness, it might be making it work where is comfortable. We have read of mothers who have been confined to their beds and have done a majority of their schooling and reading assignments with their kids sitting on the bed with them. Make it and take it where it works for you.

A great way to do nature study during a crisis, or even when things are going well, is to have a backpack ready to go with any supplies you might like to take with you. Supplies might include paper, nature notebooks, colored pencils, watercolors, paint brushes, a bottle of water—or even better, paint brush pens that already have water inside them—a roll of paper towels, magnifying glasses, a portable microscope, and snacks— anything you might want to be able to just quickly grab and go could go into the backpack that could become your nature knapsack. What an easy way to head out the door and enjoy some nature in the midst of what you are going through.

What it comes down to is that we need to give ourselves grace to do the important things in the middle of a crisis, so we can make it to the other side. To just do the things will keep us moving forward and keep our families cared for and safe. Years ago, one of our pastors talked about how to get through a storm, or crisis, in your life: in the middle of it, you should just keep doing the basic things you know to do. That's it. The basics.

THINGS I WANT TO REMEMBER...

LIFE-GIVING

"Giving life or spirit; having power to give life; inspiriting; invigorating."
(Webster's Revised Unabridged Dictionary)

Chapter 7: *Teach the Whole Person*

Chapter 8: *More than Academics*

Chapter 9: *Bonded for Life*

TEACH THE WHOLE PERSON 

One of our favorite homeschooling writers and podcasters is Sally Clarkson. She and her husband, Clay, have homeschooled all four of their children, who are now grown adults. They have continued to be influential and speak into the lives of other moms and homeschooling parents. They have done a beautiful job sharing their story about how they created their homeschooling life. One of their very first decisions was to determine what their family values would be. They have done this well, but they didn't keep it a secret. They then shared it with families around the world, encouraging us to "teach the whole person."

In this chapter, we would like to share ways that you can teach every facet of your child—spirit, soul, and body. Education is more than just academic learning, but it is acquiring knowledge and wisdom in each area of our lives. In each of the segments that follow, we want to address them first to the parents, so the parents can then educate their children. We know, in order for our children to truly absorb what we are teaching them, we must model it. We must lead them by our example—do what we do and not just what we say. We are saying to them, "Let's do this together!"

What is our spirit? According to Vocabulary.com, "Spirit comes from the Latin word for 'breath,' and like breath, spirit is considered a fundamental part of being alive." Our spirit is our inmost being, and it is the part of us that makes us alive. Without spirit, we wouldn't have a soul, and our body would die. Spirit is the central part of our being.

How, then, do we feed and build up our spirit that we cannot see, and what does that even mean? Just as our physical bodies can be weakened or made stronger, so can our spirit become weak. To build up our spirits, we must input the right information. The saying "garbage in, garbage out" is true. For those who are operating from a Christian perspective, studying the Bible is one of the key methods to teach our children, and it builds up both their spirits and ours at the same time. We see this happen in a couple of different ways during our homeschooling days.

First of all, we have scriptures we memorize. We learn a new verse every so often, and we practice all of the verses, and the new verse we are learning, at least five days a week. As we learn the verses, it helps us meditate on what they say and how to put them into practice for our lives—what they truly mean to us and for us. Next, we study the Bible as part of our "nucleus." We take portions of the scripture and read it together. We talk about what it means and make notes, so we can refer back to the discussion, and we talk about how we can apply it to our daily lives. How can your family do that with what you believe? Strengthening our inner man is what will help us, and our children, navigate through life in a healthy manner.

Our soul, which is comprised of our mind, will, and emotions, also needs to be fed on a regular basis.

First of all, our mind needs to have living ideas presented to it. Living ideas are something with which you can form a connection; you can make a long-term association, rather than a short-term memorization. You are able to take a thought and link it to something else in your mind.

For the sake of illustration, let us pretend you have a bulletin board, like our son does—for him it is his "spy board"—and on it, you have placed a picture of someone. Then, somewhere else on the board, you have a picture of someone else, and another picture and another picture. They are secured with thumbtacks, and you take a piece of yarn from the first picture, and you connect it with the second picture, and then, it goes to the third picture, and so on. It is visually showing us how these people relate to each other. That is the same concept as when we talk about living ideas and how one thought connects to a different one. As we teach our children, our goal is to help them link together what is being taught.

Here is an example from a few years ago, when we specifically remember watching our children build a relationship with a living idea. We had read about the "Brave 300", and they began to use that in their play time. One child acted out the part of King Leonidas, leader of the Greek army of 300 in the Battle of Thermopylae. The other child was part of the army, and they were fighting for their freedom to the death against a massive, Persian army. The courage of the Greeks in the face of such an overwhelming opposition was an inspiration to our children. The outcome wasn't good for the Greeks, but they stood for what they believed in, thus teaching our children about patriotism and bravery. We were privy to observe this without them noticing us. It was enjoyable to see them take what they were taught and put it into practice. They made a connection.

We also need to help direct their will. We tend to think of a strong-willed child being one who pulls against us. However, it has been said that when children resist instruction, they are actually weak-willed. Being weak-willed means that one can know the right thing to do but does not do it. Having a strong will, therefore, shows self-control and a resolve to do the right thing. In order to instill and build strong wills in our children, we need to help them form good and healthy habits. This takes consistency and patience. Over time, however, helping them develop healthy habits will pay off in the formation of good character if we don't give up.

Finally, the third part of our soul is our emotions. Feelings are created by God; however, some feelings should not be allowed to take up residency. They should be visitors only and not take up residency. We have to be able to teach our children that it is okay to feel certain emotions, but we do not have to act on each emotion that we feel. For example, both Shala and our youngest child have anger issues. She has resolved to talk it out with him when she is feeling that tension inside herself, so she can teach him it is okay to feel that emotion—but she can walk in self-control and not give in to anger. This has been a great teaching tool in our home to better direct our reactions and responses.

BODY

The final component to teaching the whole person is making sure that we are including our bodies in the process. It can be so easy to find ourselves eating unhealthy food, because it can be the easiest to grab when we are spending a majority of our time at home. It can also be challenging to get our bodies moving and making sure that we remain active. Sometimes, it feels easier to stay in our slouchy clothes than to put on what we need to get out the door and have some physical activity that is fun.

A former homeschooling mom has challenged Shala to take care of her body both in nutrition and in physical activity, so she can be healthy. It isn't necessarily about losing weight—although that might be needed—but it is primarily about our overall health. This sets the example for our children about keeping our bodies moving and eating nutritious foods. The Bible tells us that our bodies are temples, and we are to take care of them, because they don't belong to us: they belong to God (1 Corinthians 6:19-20). We want to bring our best to God in other areas, so we should also make sure we are bringing our best to Him when it comes to our bodies.

Some ways to work on this is through fun activities. It is amazing what happens when you send, or take, the kids out to play in the backyard and how creative and active they can be with their playtime. Blow some bubbles together and chase them. Play tag or hide-and-seek. You can also visit a playground or have them participate in organized sports. Go bicycling through the neighborhood or on a trail. It can be going on a hike together, and then, if you add in a nature walk portion with that, you can get a two-for-one time of learning. Find enjoyable ways to get your bodies active, such as dancing around the house on a rainy day or heading outside with your rain boots on to jump in the puddles. The kids love it when we get active with them. Find ways of enjoyment that work for your family and have fun together. Added benefits are laughing together and knowing that we are making memories that will be treasured.

In essence, we have the best job in the world as parent educators. We get to pour our values into our children. We get to see them learn and grow in areas in which they excel and see them grow up in areas that aren't as exciting for them. We get to see them flourish as they read living books that give them living ideas. We get to spend time hanging out and being with them. What an incredible opportunity we have to teach the whole person of our child.

CHAPTER 8

MORE THAN ACADEMICS

We want to remind you that homeschooling is not just about academics, and that is one reason that makes it so great. It is about so much more! One of our greatest joys is seeing when our children are learning beyond what we can teach them academically. Anything from riding a bike to an area of passion—such as woodworking, sewing, or mechanics—to learning how to run a business, because they are entrepreneurially-minded. We want to share with you some ideas for how you can make this happen based on what we and other homeschooling families are doing.

FOCUS ON LIFE SKILLS

Life skills are a great way to focus on education. Enlist the help of your children to a greater degree in the home and teach them things you need help with that would also benefit them as they are going through life. It could be as simple as teaching them how to do laundry, cook a meal, budget, or service a car. It may be educating them in things—like computer coding, photography, or other such items—that would be interesting to your child, while not necessarily beneficial to your family at the time, it can be a fun activity that can produce great results later in his or her life.

For those of you who may hope that your children learn certain life skills that you don't have, we want to ask, "Have you heard about the 'Dad, how do I?' YouTube channel that became an overnight sensation in 2020?" His premise is that his dad left him at the age of 12, and he didn't have anyone to teach him certain life skills, so he had to learn on his own. He then put on his creative hat and decided to help others who also may not have the information as to how to do certain things. He talks about various tools, he even reads books to his viewers and tells jokes, shows how to tie a tie, as well as how to shave, how to build a bench, put up a shelf, and how to fix things—such as running toilets and clogged bathtubs. YouTube can be a great resource for teaching specific skills we don't have, but we desire to pass along to our children.

Similar to teaching them life skills and involving them in the work process, you can ask them or at least observe areas of passion they have and begin to work with them in developing those areas.

INVOLVE YOUR KIDS IN THE PROCESS

We absolutely love getting our children involved with us in work and ministry. We are self-employed and have been for over 10 years now—operating a local newspaper turned magazine—and we love that they get to be involved in various aspects. At times, when we have had inserts to put into the newspaper, we have taught them how to do piece work and been able to pay them for their services; it gave them experience by being a part of the process—plus, it helped us. Now that we operate a magazine, one of our children absolutely loves photography, and she is able to utilize her skills and build her portfolio by taking pictures that we then highlight in the magazine. In addition to involving our children with our work, we have involved them in ministry with us at our church over the course of their lives in one way or another. This type of education goes beyond what formal academics can teach them. While we know that not everybody's family situation looks like ours, we would definitely encourage and challenge you to find ways your children can work alongside you with what you are doing.

One mother we talked to recently was having a get-together with other homeschooling families at a park. She wanted a nice poster-board sign made, so they could be located easily. She involved her six-year old daughter by asking her to make the sign. She was ecstatic about being a part of the planning, and it was a simple way for her to be engaged.

Involving your children can be as simple as having a conversation on their level about what is going on in family life. Even as we have struggled in our financial situation at times, we have tried to use that as a teaching time to show them what we have done wrong, how we could do things better, talk about where we are, and why maybe they cannot have a certain item purchased for them at this time. This helps to begin the process of building a greater understanding in them as to how to make some of the "not-so-easy" choices. We don't lay the full heavy burden on them; however, we do try and take certain circumstances and teach them in an appropriate way at their level.

From time to time, we also involve our children in the process of determining what should be included in their education. Not that we make education child-centric; however, it is nice to hear from their point of view what they would like to learn or in what areas they would like to participate. This can give a good direction for those who are unschooling, or it can help direct in the afternoons during the times of "relaxed productivity"—see chapter two for more information on these homeschooling methods. We have also added in some of their input from time to time to our morning learning schedule that is a bit more formal in nature.

STARTING THEIR OWN BUSINESS OR ENTERING THE WORK FORCE

One thing that we have noticed about homeschooling families is that they encourage their children in entrepreneurial ways or in other forms of employment. Even during the younger years, children who are interested in starting a business can begin to read books about how to do so, put together a simple business plan, and can actually start some form of a business in which they are interested. This can be used as part of their schooling experience. We also used a business math course for our daughter when she was in sixth grade. She ran her own hypothetical bookstore. This was not only better for her academically, because she was less-than-thrilled about having to do math, but it also encouraged her entrepreneurial spirit and what it looks like to own her own business, and therefore, provided her with real life experience as to why math is necessary.

Our youngest wanted to have a lemonade stand. It seems fun when you see it on television. We were able to talk him into selling ice-cold bottled water instead, because it was logistically more feasible. We helped him think through what he would need to begin—a table, sign, start-up cash, bottled water he needed to refrigerate, an ice chest with ice to keep the water cold, a chair, and something to entertain himself while he sat outside. Within 20 minutes, he wanted to come back inside. We encouraged him to stay outside a bit longer. One sale was all it took, and he was hooked. He kept going out, day after day, during the hot summer to sell his bottled water. People would come by just to compliment him on his hard work. At the age of nine, this was a great learning experience for him—how to operate his own business and the value of hard work.

Kids going into the upper levels of school, depending on their age, can begin to seek out employment opportunities and use that as part of their school day, plus it is also a way to put money into their pockets. This can teach a good work ethic, is a great time to begin or continue teaching about budgeting, and can be a great way to supplement their days. It adds value to their future résumé and possibly their college application—if they choose to go this route.

GET OUT OF THE HOUSE

Field Trips

We were recently reminded by our daughter about how getting out of the house and going to visit various places is a huge part of our learning experience. Education doesn't just take place at home, but can be greatly enhanced by going on field trips as a family, and even with other homeschooling families. A field trip could be as simple as going to the library, or it could capitalize on what is being learned in school, because maybe there is a museum or other such places to visit that are close by, and what is being studied can be observed firsthand. Field trips can also be done within your home by visiting places via YouTube channels or videos on Amazon Prime. Recently, we checked out a book about the national parks, and then would connect it with short videos we found on Amazon Prime about the same national parks. This was a fun activity and went beyond just our academic learning, so we could go places without traveling anywhere.

Nature Study

As we have discussed in earlier chapters, getting outside in nature is one of the simplest ways to get out of the house. There are a couple of ways to do this. First, you can do a simple nature walk, which is at it sounds: a walk in nature with little to no teaching. A second way is to do a nature study, which involves taking what is seen in nature and studying it more. Regardless, our children need to be enjoying the fresh air, noticing the detail of creation, and learning how to train the eye to observe and see precisely what is going on. It is also beneficial for us parents to get outdoors to aid the health of our mind and body. It gives us a chance to model ways for our children to observe nature and to enjoy being outside—in the backyard, at a nature reserve, a park, or wherever you can make this happen. It's a bit harder in a city setting, but it still can be doable.

We have been encouraged by one of the homeschool bloggers that we follow, Erika Alicea from Charlotte Mason City Living, about how she and her daughter are able to be out in nature, even in a busy city. Here are some ideas: "Start by exploring your neighborhood"—there is nature among buildings and flowers can grow out of cracks in the sidewalk. "Visit parks and community gardens"—look at the dirt, find a worm, watch the birds, study the insects, find different kinds of rocks, observe the flowers and trees. We even have a portable microscope and magnifying glass that we sometimes bring along. "Bring nature study into your home" by planting an indoor garden of flowers, plants, or herbs, or watch a caterpillar grow and then metamorphosize into a butterfly and release it, which we and many other families have done. Other recommendations are to visit preset places that have nature built into them, such as zoos and botanical gardens. Also, consider joining an already established nature group or start one of your own. There are many ways to observe and take part in nature, if we will slow down and be intentional about looking at nature.

We need to take our children, and not just send them, outside. We understand there are times when parents need to be working inside, and kids need to be playing outside; however, we need to be more purposeful about being in the great outdoors with them. This shouldn't be a strict teaching time, when we plan every moment and try to entertain our children. We should allow nature, exploration, and the creativity in our children to be their focus. We can take time to point things out, so our children can see what we are talking about in greater detail. We can teach them, and learn right alongside them. For those unsure of what things are named or how to identify them, we recommend grabbing some field guides and taking them along with you. One of our greatest activities has been inside our home watching the bird feeder outside the dining room window. We have a local field guide on birds (*Birds of Connecticut Field Guide*), and we observe the birds and go to the field guide to see and name what they are and to find out more detail about them. We also have a foldable pocket field guide for trees and wildflowers (*Connecticut Trees and Wildflowers*) for when we are out and about, so we can determine what species we are seeing. And, we recently added the *National Audubon Society Field Guide to North American Insects and Spiders*, so we can figure out what bugs are in our yard.

Recently, a tropical storm moved through our area, and we were cleaning up the leaves and noticed we have two different types of oak trees. Up until this point, we knew we had oak trees, but never looked closely to see if we had more than one kind. We looked at the clumps of leaves and the ends of some were pointed, while others were rounded. We opened our field guide and found out that we have both white oak and red oak trees. This was a simple, yet fun, time spent observing our environment in more detail.

We have also found it fascinating to observe nature by raising our own chickens. We got them when they were two days old, and now, they are egg-producing hens. We also have cousins who raise bunnies and brush out their fur to use for needle felting projects.

As you can see, there are many ways in which a family can observe and study nature. Different times in our lives, as well as the different seasons throughout the year, will affect what this looks like.

Meetups

As we talked about in chapter three about finding people to support you, just getting out of the house to meet up with other homeschoolers is necessary—not just for the kids, but also for the parents to be able to interact. Recently, we attended a gathering for parents interested in homeschooling their kids during the upcoming school year. We found it refreshing to be able to interact with other parents making similar choices. We could relate and share experiences and information with those who "get us." Not only did our kids have fun playing together, but we came away from this time feeling refreshed. Meetups can be a simple get-together at a park or home, or they can be as structured as a homeschool co-op. Whichever direction you take, it is nice to get out the door and not be solely focused on the academics of our children. There are additional things to learn, such as how to interact with others, how to respond when things don't go as planned—such as when there isn't a playground at the location you chose to meet and they are disappointed;

this can be a time of creatively figuring out what to do—how to pack a picnic lunch, and a variety of things that may be specific to your family.

Like we said at the beginning of this chapter, education is much more than just academics. Learning should be happening in every aspect of our lives. With whomever and wherever we are. Each moment has the capability to be an experiential learning time for our kids—with and without us actually teaching them. We are born to learn, so let's have fun doing it together.

CHAPTER 9

BONDED FOR LIFE

We know that when we look at Instagram, Facebook, and other types of social media, we are seeing the highlight reels of other families. However, one thing we have noticed in face-to-face interactions, as well as what we have seen online, is for most homeschooling families, there is an immense connection. There are families of all sizes—from an only child to those with many children—and for the most part, there is a bond which is intense and stays in the families even after the children have grown and are out of the house.

We have friends who homeschooled, and now their kids are out of the house and married—some with children of their own—yet they are still tight knit. Clay and Sally Clarkson, as we have talked about before, home educated their now-grown children, and they have a strong friendship bond, which seems to be without rival. As our own children are growing up, we have seen the friendships grow between us and them—not to the extent that we can't still operate as their parents—and we have seen the friendship continue to build between them as siblings. It is a beautiful aspect of homeschool life, to be able to not only learn together, but to form what we hope to be a lasting bond of friendship within our family.

We don't mean for this to be a weird sense of being bonded, but as we go through life and families don't necessarily stay in a close geographic location, the ability to rely on each other for friendship and stability is comforting. In the current days of technology, it is easier than ever to stay connected on a regular basis. We need each other.

As we have gone through ups and downs, moves, and crises, one of the greatest things for us is that we have been able to lean on each other, knowing we will always—as much as is within our power—be there for each other. It brings a sense of peace to know we are in this together, we will get through this together, and then, we will come out on the other side together. We understand that sometimes, there are things outside of our control, such as a family member dying, but the commitment is foundational that we will stay together as best we can.

At the time of writing this book, we are considering a move from the Northeast to the Midwest—to be closer to extended family, along with other reasons—but who knows if that will actually happen. It is a bit nerve-wracking to think of changing locations after being here over ten years, but knowing that we have each other brings a level of peace that we otherwise wouldn't have.

Recently, Shala had a moment at bedtime when she was in real need of a friend, a woman friend. With there being no one around and knowing that our 12-year-old daughter was still awake, reading, she took the opportunity to go into her room and have some girl time. They talked, shared, laughed, and probably cried. It was a refreshing time, and it was great that this moment could be shared between mom and daughter. They also take time to go out and have "afternoon tea" and enjoy shopping together. Our nine-year-old son loves throwing the baseball with dad and desires to go "on a date" with mom from time to time. We believe that seizing these opportunities at their ages now will form a long-term friendship with our kids.

Close friends of ours homeschooled their daughter until high school. Sometime during that season, they drifted apart, but in recent years, their relationship has been restored. There is hope by planting the right seeds now, even if they go down a path we don't desire for them, they will come back home. We are glad that it doesn't have to be us, the parents, and them, the kids, but we can be in this time together…as a family.

SIBLINGS

We love stories, and here is one more from our family. One day, on the way to softball practice, our daughter was talking about her relationship with her brother. She mentioned she enjoys that wherever we go, even if they don't know anyone, they have each other. We have also watched them spend day after day playing together. Not that they are with each other all the time, but they have a good mix of spending time doing things together: sometimes, they are doing separate things but in the same room, and other times, they are having moments of doing things by themselves.

Shala also recalls when she and her older brother went to an overnight camp for a week each summer. She was nervous on most of these occasions, but what really helped was knowing that her brother was there. There is something about knowing you have someone to lean on in potentially unsettling circumstances—someone in your corner.

For larger families we have talked to, during the day—whether it be school time or open time—the older children tend to help the younger ones.

This not only helps Mom, who is doing the main job of homeschooling and running the home in these circumstances, but it gives the younger ones someone to look up to. Many times, the younger ones are willing to do and learn things just because they want to emulate the older kids.

We believe these relationships can be cultivated when families aren't going different directions from morning until night. Homeschooling makes this possible.

Yes, there are those families in which there is an only child. Obviously, sibling relationships won't be there, but it can still be a time of connecting with parents and extended family, and that is what we are going to chat about next.

EXTENDED FAMILY

That brings us to the extended family—grandparents, aunts, uncles, cousins, and such. We have lived far away from most of our extended family, and homeschooling has afforded us the opportunity to visit them at various times throughout the years, especially when the cost is the lowest and places aren't as packed as when public and private schools are out of session. There is much wisdom that can be gleaned from being with older family members, and we want to have good memories of them when they are gone. It is more difficult for that to happen if we don't spend time with them. Our goal is for our kids to truly know them. Your goals may vary, or you may be estranged from other family members, but we truly hope that you can connect with and enjoy being around the family that God gave you.

In addition to building relationships with our extended family, they can be a part of the educational process. We have friends who live far away from their grandparents, but the grandma is a former math teacher. She will be doing a majority of the math teaching with the grandkids, via Zoom or FaceTime. Therefore, she is a part of the process, building relationships with her grandkids, and it is also a stress reliever for the parents by having someone who has the expertise needed in a particular subject.

However, if your extended family doesn't get to be a part of your time together, we hope that you will seek to "make" your own extended family —with close friends and those about whom you care and love.

In a question-and-answer session done by Erica Lamberg for *Ladders*, she asked Peter Lovenheim, author of *The Attachment Effect: Exploring the Powerful Ways Our Earliest Bond Shapes Our Relationships and Lives*, about how bonding and attachment affect us into adulthood. His response is that having a secure attachment as a child makes all the difference in having trusting relationships, coping with stress, and doing well in the workplace as adults.

Therefore, one of the keys to our children being successful in going out into the world is their secure attachment at home, and we have the ability to make that happen now. From the earliest of ages, children start to venture off, but need to know they have someone to run back to. They do this often. They go play, and then return. They venture farther, and then come back and find us, the parents, still there. As they enter adulthood, and move forward in life, they need to have the security that we, as parents, and their siblings will always be there for them. Let's help them become successful by creating a nurturing and bonded family in which they can grow.

THINGS I WANT TO REMEMBER...

PEOPLE

"Men, women, and children."
(Cambridge Dictionary)

Chapter 10: *Develop Relationships with*

People of All Ages and Stages

Chapter 11: *Raise Informed Citizens*

Chapter 12: *Cultivate World Changers*

DEVELOP RELATIONSHIP WITH PEOPLE OF ALL AGES AND STAGES

One of the most common questions we get asked when people find out we homeschool is, "What about socialization?" If you ask other homeschooling families, they will tell you this is one of the top questions they receive, as well. We polled our Instagram tribe, and here are some of the ways they have responded to others when asked the same question.

"I'll usually ask how their kids socialize, which in turn leads to a lot of 'we do that, too' from me."

"I simply ask, 'What about it?' And then, the conversation typically moves on, because I don't think most people who asked the question even know why they're asking."

"Usually, I'm getting a compliment on how sweet and well-behaved my boys are, and I say, 'Thanks. That's homeschool socialization for ya!'"

We believe that one conversation starter with others can be to teach others what socialization really is. When they ask us about socialization, they are really meaning, "What kind of interactions are they getting with their peers?" However, if we look up the definition of socialization, here is what it really means. The Merriam-Webster Dictionary says socialization is "the process beginning during childhood by which individuals acquire the values, habits, and attitudes of a society." Now, we would ask if children can only acquire the right values, habits, and attitudes needed for use in society only by being with their peers? We believe that most would answer, "No."

True socialization requires being around people of various ages and in different life stages—those older, younger, and the same age as our children—to instill in our children the right, courteous, and respectful ways to respond in various situations in society. Also being around different races and cultures is beneficial, so they can understand that socialization—values, habits, and attitudes—can look differently, depending upon where and with whom we are interacting—what is acceptable in certain parts of the United States, might not be accepted as the societal norm in Ethiopia.

So, we can see that when asked about socialization, most people are concerned about our children not receiving enough friend time. For those who have already begun to homeschool, we know that it is what we make it. Personally, we choose for them to regularly be around friends in church, sports, music, and other various activities. It may not be having friend time "at school," but most of the time, we are able to offer them plenty of time with their peers, plus time to learn how to interact with their elders and those younger than them.

Now, let's look at what can be learned by interacting with mentors, peers, and mentees.

I want to begin with talking about what our children can learn from their peers, since this is the primary concern of those who don't understand the homeschooling scene. By collaborating with their peers in a play or academic environment, students are able to work primarily on the same level and critique and evaluate each other, even though they may not know they're doing it. It can feel like a less threatening environment, because they are giving and receiving feedback by those on their own level.

Obviously, it doesn't mean that our children's friends are experts in what we are trying to teach them; however, they are able to learn how to get along, how to share their toys or other items, and how to communicate. We have watched our younger children interact with their peers in a variety of situations. It is amazing to watch and listen to their conversations that we think are extremely basic and weird, but because they are interacting with their peers who have a similar mindset and interests, the conversation is perfectly normal to them.

Most homeschooling parents do understand the need for their children to be around other kids, and therefore, will find groups for interaction. It might be a co-op or playdate. It might be having them involved in sporting activities. There are a variety of ways for our children to engage with others their age, and it does not have to be in a school environment. Parents just need to figure out what works for their family and find those activities that are conducive to providing these types of relationships.

A benefit of being around their friends is peer learning. Potentially, one friend will have an interest in an area the other friend may not have as much knowledge about that subject. They can learn from each other.

It can help the one who knows the material already gain a greater understanding of it, and it can aid the one learning the information by it being relayed on a level that is understandable. One of the pitfalls, however, that can be seen is that misinformation may be passed along as factual. Also we, as parents, need to make sure they're learning good stuff, and not things we deem harmful to our children, but we should be monitoring that anyway, as they are going through life and learning from various means.

MENTORS

Not only do our children interact with their peers when they are being homeschooled, they have the opportunity to interact with various adults. They should be learning how to speak respectfully and honoring those who are older than them, whether it be siblings, family members, or adults. They are able to observe and learn by being around those older than them about how to act in certain situations. They can also gain knowledge and information they are not learning at home, because they are around other adults who specialize in certain fields of study.

Mentors, teachers, professionals, and those with experience in specialties our children wish to learn, can be sought out to help them progress in areas of interest. These individuals are in addition to those everyday mentors—parents, family, and friends—who are able to instill into our children the values, character, and habits we desire for them.

Finally, our children also need to have those into whom they are pouring value; these are known as mentees. They don't even need to be very old to begin this process. If you have more than one child in your family, then your older children, regardless of their ages, are able to impact their younger siblings' lives. They can teach simple things, like how to set the table, how to do laundry, how to have a better attitude, how to write, how to read to each other, and much more. As we have attended various homeschooling functions, our children have interacted with other kids of various ages and have been able to influence them, hopefully, for the better. Basically, as long as they are one step ahead of others, they can become a mentor to others they are around. Having those they are mentoring aids in teaching our children they are not the center of the world. It helps them overcome selfishness, see the needs others have, and walk in compassion.

We, as humans, are definitely not meant to be isolated from each other. Socializing and connection are important for emotional stability and growth. Just as we talked about the importance of community and support in chapter three, this subject of socialization falls in line with that, as well. Not just for the fact of having friends and relationships, but because they help us grow.

CHAPTER 11

RAISE INFORMED CITIZENS

The study of civics—including citizenship, U.S. history, and the study of local, state, and federal government—is part of the required curriculum that must be completed in order to graduate from a U.S. high school, whether homeschool, public, or private. Civics is the study of the rights and duties of a citizen: one who is either born in a country or becomes a part of that country. In order to understand what our rights and privileges are and what we owe our country, students must study our history to find out from where we have come and how our country came to be.

In a *Washington Examiner* article from 2011, according to a study done by Intercollegiate Studies Institute, a survey done in 85 colleges and with 28,000 American college students showed that the average score on a 60-question basic civic test was 54-percent. That is a less-than-passing grade.

In 2003, Dr. Brian Ray of NHERI.org, in conjunction with HSLDA.org, conducted a study of homeschoolers who were now adults. He found that 4.2 percent of homeschool graduates felt that politics and government were too challenging to comprehend versus 35-percent of adults who were educated by other means. In addition, 76-percent of those who were age 18 to 24 and homeschooled, compared to 29-percent of the same age demographic and schooled by other means, had voted within the past five years.

So, even though civics is a required subject in high school, the majority of graduates still have little knowledge of what it is and how they can be a good, involved citizen. What does it mean to be a good citizen? The consensus of traits one should possess are: patriotism (love of country), contributing member of society, good character (trustworthy, honest, compassionate, full of integrity, and kindness), active in the community, well-informed, vigilant, participative in the political process (voting), obedient to laws and authority, respectful of the rights of others, tolerant (not tolerance unless you disagree with me—we can agree to disagree), and just.

With that said, we believe an immense benefit of homeschooling is to instill in our children a desire and knowledge of how to be involved in positive ways in society. How can we, as homeschool parents, make sure that our children are informed citizens? Here are some simple, yet effective, ways in which you can proceed to make this happen.

EDUCATE

The main way we should teach our children is to just talk with them. Have conversations about what makes a good citizen and how to be an active participant in the community and, ultimately, the nation. We take time to talk about what is going on in our government nationally, statewide, and locally at the dinner table, while driving in the car, and any other chance we get. Sometimes, the kids have been thinking about what is going on and come up with their own questions for us. If we don't know the answer, we will look it up together. Otherwise, we respond and let them continue thinking about what we said. It is great for them to try and think through and digest what we are teaching them.

We also learn about current events and talk about what they mean for us. It is important for us to discuss what is going on in society and how it relates to our freedom and rights, and what we can do to make a difference. Being silent isn't a good option. Either our children will hear what is going on from others and will likely turn to that viewpoint, or we can share with them on their level and integrate what we believe into the conversation.

They also listen to us while we talk about state homeschooling laws and guidelines and the difference between the two—as well as the difference in each state's laws. It is nice to see them learning through normal, everyday occurrences of issues that affect us as citizens, and more specifically, as a homeschooling family.

Another creative and fun way we learn together is through the "Election Night Board Game." We play and talk, while laughing and being competitive, about what each of the aspects of a presidential election is. It brings a greater understanding of the way government works in a unique way.

We also study living, historical books—see chapter two as to what a "living book" is—to see "the good, the bad, and the ugly" of what has happened, so certain parts of history might not repeat themselves. Plus, we can see how things have developed over time and the best ways that citizens have created lasting change in history, so we can determine how best to see justice happen in society.

And, we enjoy talking about famous historical figures who were home educated such as: Benjamin Franklin; former Presidents Abraham Lincoln, Franklin Delano Roosevelt, James Madison, and George Washington; Alexander Graham Bell, who invented the telephone; Eli Whitney, who invented the cotton gin; and Orville and Wilbur Wright, who built the first successful airplane.

Education must go beyond just talking and reading about it, but we must teach our children to participate in what our nation is doing. From our earliest memories of having our younger children, we have taken them along with us to vote. They sometimes even get an "I Voted" sticker, which means the world to them. They get to see us participating in our civic duty, and it encourages them to be a part of the process when they become of age.

In addition, one of our favorite things to do is to join with one of our homeschool groups that hosts an annual Capitol Day, where we homeschoolers get to converge *en masse* on the State Capitol, meet with our legislators, take a tour of the capitol building while learning about our state's history, and discover such things as how a bill becomes a law.

We also know that, as parents, we set the example for children. If we want them to participate in civic duties, then we must go before them. Chris, for instance, has served on the town council. Shala has been involved with the local Rotary Club and participated in community outreach through them. We also participate by voting and taking the kids along, so they can see the process. In order for us to strongly encourage our children to be civic-minded, we need to model that behavior for them.

In addition, one of the ways for them to be a patriot of our country is for us to show them how much we love our country; we must also talk about the freedoms we have and how those came to be.

Other families have been involved in peaceful protests and respectful marches, such as in the pro-life movement. They have been teaching their children effective ways to make changes in our country, and some have even included their children in these events with them.

In the *Washington Examiner* article we referenced in our opening paragraphs in this chapter, Dr. Rich Brake concluded that those who are able and willing to self-educate, tend to be more involved in civic duties, community events, and government issues. As homeschooling parents, one of our main goals should be to teach our children how to educate themselves, so they become lifelong learners. This seems to be key among those who are more active in a positive way in our country.

CHAPTER 12
CULTIVATE WORLD CHANGERS

We have a strong desire for our children to make a difference in the world. It may not be the entire world, but at least the portion of it in which they interact. One of the basic ways to do that is to teach our children to care—about God, people, society, and our country. That isn't done strictly through academics or by happenstance, but by us intentionally caring and passing that along to our children. Charlotte Mason said, "The question is not, 'how much does the youth know?' when he has finished his education, but, 'how much does he care?' and, 'about how many orders of things does he care?' In fact, 'how large is the room in which he finds his feet set?' and, 'therefore, how full is the life he has before him?'" We want to be able to say, and hope that our children join along with us, "I C.A.R.E." But how do we make that happen?

CAUSE

The first step we would like to encourage you in is to find a cause, even when your children are small, that you and your family can believe in and get behind. As the children get older, they will begin to have a sense as to various causes they would like to support. For example, our son has always been tender-hearted towards animals, and recently shared with us, at the whopping age of nine, that he would like to operate a pet rescue organization when he gets older. He is our child who very much knows his mind, and when he makes it up to do something, he will do it. So, for the current time, since he has this interest and passion, one way to channel it is to participate at a local pet shelter that will allow a child of his age to come in, along with us as his parents, to participate in some of the needs they have, such as helping clean.

A quick search of the Internet will showcase a variety of kid-friendly causes in which they can be involved, such as raising money for clean water wells in third world countries, gathering and donating groceries to a food bank, and becoming involved with organizations that help supply vitamins and medical care to other children in need are just a few to be named.

You can also encourage an older child to research and study about a need and what is the most beneficial way to meet it.

ACTION

Once your children are old enough to begin taking some action on their own, you can sit down with them and begin to develop an action plan of what they can do even now to further the cause in which they believe. Using our son's example about helping rescue pets, the process could begin as simple as learning how to care for a pet in your home, finding out how best to volunteer and get others to be a part of that process, and deciding about how and where to receive donations, monetary or products. It could also include what they want to see done within the next week, month, three months, or one year. By helping them find practical steps and plan out their goals, they can become more successful in making a difference.

Just as when adults start their own business, they need to build a business plan, so on a simpler scale, we can help create an action plan with our children. We need to help them think through how to make their desire to help a cause become a reality.

Once you and your children have determined your cause and created an action plan, or even while you are in the midst of doing so, it is very important to discuss that their part matters. It doesn't matter their age or anything else. There is only one of them, and they were placed on this earth as the only one able to fulfill a specific role. We, as their parents, are to teach them what responsibility means—how to do what needs to be done, when it needs to be done—as well as that they have a responsibility to make a difference in the world in which they live.

In talking to our son about the part he can play in rescuing pets, we encourage him that his desire is valid and good. We talk about how it will make a difference in the life of each pet with which he works. It is like the starfish story, where one person on a beach sees a whole bunch of starfish that cannot get back into the ocean. An onlooker notices that the person takes a starfish and throws it back in to the water. They do this time and time again. The onlooker mentions there are too many of them to really make a difference. The person then picks up a starfish, throws it in, and says it made a difference for that one. We have the opportunity to teach our children that even what seems like a small difference is still our responsibility to make happen.

Endurance is a necessary quality to instill in our children. While it may not be a trait that is prevalent in our society today, we can choose to make this part of their home education. We can teach them to be in something for the long haul. To make a commitment and follow through. To be tenacious. To never give up, even when it's hard. It's easy to get tired when we aren't seeing results, but if it's truly a cause to fight for and to make happen, then we must model and teach our kids how to continue, even when things are harder than expected. The Bible says in 1 Corinthian 15:58 (NLT), "So, my dear brothers and sisters, be strong and immovable. Always work enthusiastically for the Lord, for you know that nothing you do for the Lord is ever useless." Coupled with endurance, we must also work with joy and hope. What we are doing isn't a waste of time if we are called to do the work.

For our son, we can teach him that what he is currently learning about pet care is a part of who he is and can be useful in the future. If he is faithful in taking care of his pets now, then we can build upon that as he gets older with more of what he desires to pursue. Just because he doesn't "feel" like seeing something through, doesn't mean he should shirk his responsibility. Commitment must run deeper than our ever-changing feelings.

A REAL LIFE EXAMPLE

While writing this chapter, we actually sat down with our 12-year-old daughter to create an I C.A.R.E. plan, and here is the outcome:

Cause. First off, we discussed various areas of passion—reading, history, eating, hanging out with friends, and playing sports. We then asked if she had any causes about which she was interested. She mentioned getting others involved in reading and clean water wells being dug around the world. We settled on the cause for this season of her life being about digging clean water wells in third world countries. Next, we located an organization that was already doing what she wanted to see done and with which it would be good to be connected. We settled on charity: water. Her next step is to educate herself about the cause. To study and know what the statistics are and why the need is great. She needs to research and get the necessary knowledge, so she can share with others. Plus, she will be determining how best to utilize her photography skills for this cause.

Action. In talking through the first steps of an action plan, we brainstormed ideas of what it might entail. Here are some ideas. She would want to put together a booth to show the need for clean water—both in-person and virtual. In-person booths would include showing samples of dirty water in water bottles, a display of statistics of why clean water is necessary, and a chosen location for the well to be dug. Her virtual booth would also include pictures, videos, and a donation link directly to charity: water. She will also reach out to charity: water to see what well location she can adopt as her cause. Virtual booth ideas are to design a website and set up social media platforms (Facebook, Instagram, and Twitter).

Here is a timeline of how her action plan would be put in place. Within her first week, she plans to educate herself about the needs and statistics and look into what town on charity: water's website she would like to fund. Within her first month, she will determine what virtual platforms she plans to use and will begin setting them up—with our help, of course—as well as will talk to charity: water about what town she would like to support. Within three months, she will run between one and three in-person booths and will have been consistently working her online platforms to secure monetary donations. By the end of one year, she would like to have the well fully funded.

Responsibility. She recognizes that she can make a difference and although others are already involved in helping build clean water wells, additional people are needed to raise awareness and are needed to help secure funding. Her part matters, because she has connections with people that others might not. She can influence her corner of the world.

Endurance. We talked about how this does not have to be an ongoing, for-the-rest-of-her-life project, but that she should be committed to seeing it through completion for at least one well. Then, she can decide if it is a cause she would like to continue with, or if she would like to choose a different cause (because she has many). We are here to be her support and encourage her along the way.

We write all of this not to make life more challenging for any of us as parents, and to add more things into our already busy schedules, but to remind us, as families, to think about how to help reach out and C.A.R.E. for others—locally and worldwide. We should not be satisfied with our children simply growing up and graduating, although that is a great plan. But we should desire more for them. We should work toward them caring about changing the world in which they live.

THINGS I WANT TO REMEMBER...

SPECIAL THANKS

We want to take the time now to acknowledge those who have been instrumental in us writing this book. Special recognition goes to:

…our parents who raised us. Their impact in our lives helped shape who we are today. And, to our siblings, who have also walked this journey with us.

…our younger children, who helped along the way, prayed for us, and listened to us talk about the book over and over and over again.

…Marie Mordarski, who encouraged us, gave input into the book, helped edit it, and went on many long walks with Shala while they talked about what homeschooling families need to hear.

…Shelley Linden, who welcomed us into her homeschool group meetup as our first opportunity as The Homeschool Architects to connect with others.

…Sharon M. Johnson of WFSB Channel 3 for conducting our first television interview.

…Laura C. Cannon for our first interview for print publication.

…our Write 60 Days peeps and, more specifically, our writing accountability group comprised of Tony Pollard and Khalilah Johnson. You have helped encourage us to keep going on the days that it felt challenging to write.

…our Instagram tribe who helped by answering polls, doing interviews, and giving us ideas for content. Here they are listed by their handles:

@littlebarefootbird,
@stay.at.home.reader,
@heritagemomblog,
@little.blue.library,
@steph.and.home,
@thecircusdad,
@khalilahdjohnson,
@ourworldschoolingfamily,
@stephaniewhartonwellness,
@decemberlarks,
@theimperfecthomeschooler,
@missyb2b, and
@homeschool_mama2016.

…Joe McCullum of Eagles' Wings Business Coaching as our business coach.

…Michael D. Butler, Sr., of Beyond Publishing, and his team. Thank you for challenging Shala all those years ago to eventually write a book. And, currently, for the free writing class and the motivation to keep going to get this book printed and into the hands of soon-to-be homeschooling families. All your knowledge and expertise have been invaluable.

…our church, Vertical Church CT, and our pastors, for supporting us spiritually through this season.

…all who voted on and gave input for our book cover.

…those who have been our mentors yet probably don't even know we exist…yet, we thank you. They are Clay and Sally Clarkson, Jamie C. Martin, Sonya Schafer, Corey DeAngelis, and Kerry McDonald.

RESOURCES CITED

Alicea, Erika. "Finding Beauty Amidst Concrete." *Charlotte Mason City Living*, 3 July 2020, charlottemasoncityliving.com/finding-beauty-amidst-concrete/.

Bledsoe, Jackie. "Community Is Necessary." *Jackie Bledsoe*, 18 June 2020, www.instagram.com/jbledsoejr.

Cambridge Dictionary: Find Definitions, Meanings & Translations, dictionary.cambridge.org/us.

Clarkson, Sally. *SallyClarkson.com*, sallyclarkson.com/.

Collins, Jim. "Good Is the Enemy of Great." *Jim Collins - Video/Audio - Good Is the Enemy of Great*, 2017, www.jimcollins.com/media_topics/GoodIsTheEnemyOfGreat.html.

Crow, Mark. *Mastering Your Storms: Navigating the Trials of Life Effectively*. HonorNet, 2006.

Cui, Jiashan, and Karen Hanson. "Homeschooling in the United States: Results from the 2012 and 2016 Parent and Family Involvement Survey (PFI-NHES:2012 and 2016)." *National Center for Education Statistics (NCES) Home Page, a Part of the U.S. Department of Education*, 19 Dec. 2019, nces.ed.gov/pubsearch/pubsinfo.asp?pubid=2020001.

DeAngelis, Corey A. "Parents on Homeschooling During Coronavirus and Where They'll Send Their Kids When Schools Re-Open." *Reason Foundation*, 6 May 2020, reason.org/commentary/parents-on-homeschooling-during-coronavirus-and-where-theyll-send-their-kids-when-schools-re-open/.

"Dictionary by Merriam-Webster: America's Most-Trusted Online Dictionary." *Merriam-Webster*, Merriam-Webster, www.merriam-webster.com/.

Dictionary.com, Dictionary.com, www.dictionary.com/.

"Discover the Story of English More than 600,000 Words, over a Thousand Years." *Home : Oxford English Dictionary*, www.oed.com/.

Edited by Jamie C. Martin, *Simple Homeschool*, 8 Aug. 2020, simplehomeschool.net/.

Eisley, Loren. The Starfish Story.

"Election Night Board Game." *Amazon*, Goettsche Partners, 2011, www.amazon.com/gp/product/B07NDRRP33/ref=ppx_yo_dt_b_search_asin_title?ie=UTF8&psc=1.

Fulbright, Jeannie. "6 Ways to Spark Your Science!" *Empowering Mothers to Educate with Excellence*, 22 July 2019, www.jeanniefulbright.com/2019/05/6-ways-spark-science/.

Hollingsworth, Barbara. "Majority of American Students Flunk Civics Test." *Washington Examiner*, 5 Mar. 2011, www.washingtonexaminer.com/majority-of-american-students-flunk-civics-test.

Holy Bible: New International Version. Zondervan, 2017.

Kavanagh, James, and Raymond Leung. *Connecticut Trees and Wildflowers: an Introduction to Familiar Series*. Waterford Press, 2008.

Kenney, Rob. "Dad, How Do I?" *Practical "Dadvice" for Everyday Tasks*, YouTube, 2020, www.youtube.com/channel/UCNepEAWZH0TBu7dkxIbluDw.

Kulp, Kimberley. "Famous Homeschoolers - Who Are Famous Homeschoolers in History?" *Bridgeway*, 28 Feb. 2019, www. homeschoolacademy.com/blog/famous-homeschoolers/.

Lamberg, Erica. "New Book Says That Childhood Bonds Impact Your Career Success." *Ladders*, Ladders, 9 Oct. 2019, www.theladders. com/career-advice/new-book-says-that-childhood-bonds-impact-your-career-success.

Larson, Kent. *12 Homeschool Myths Debunked: The Book for Skeptical Dads*. Rogue School Press, 2018.

Life Application Study Bible: New Living Translation. Tyndale House Publishers, Inc., 2016.

Martin, Leah. "Moms, We Are the Home Atmosphere." *My Little Robins*, 4 Sept. 2017, mylittlerobins.com/2017/09/moms-we-are-the-home-atmosphere/.

Mason, Charlotte. *School Education*. Bottom of the Hill Publishing, 2010.

Mason, Charlotte. *Home Education*. Wilder Publications, LLC., 2008.

"Merriam-Webster Unabridged." *Merriam-Webster*, Merriam-Webster, unabridged.merriam-webster.com/.

Milne, Lorus and Margery. *National Audubon Society Field Guide to North American Insects & Spiders*. Alfred A. Knopf, 1998.

Panning, Sara Jordan. "Homeschooling with Chronic Illness." *Weird Unsocialized Homeschoolers*, 17 Aug. 2018, www. weirdunsocializedhomeschoolers.com/homeschooling-with-chronic-illness/.

Peterson, Eugene H. *The Message Bible*. NavPress, 2004.

Ray, Brian D. "Homeschooling Grows Up." *Home School Legal Defense Association*, 2003.

Schafer, Sonya. *Simply Charlotte Mason*, 14 Dec. 2008, www.youtube.com/user/SimplyCharlotteMason.

Sinek, Simon. *Start with Why*, 8 June 2020, simonsinek.com/commit/start-with-why/.

Tekiela, Stan. *Birds of Connecticut: Field Guide*. Adventure Pub., 2000.

Thinkmap, Inc. "Find out How Strong Your Vocabulary Is and Learn New Words at Vocabulary.com." *Vocabulary.com*, www.vocabulary.com/.

Zosh, Jennifer M., et al. "Learning through Play: A Review of the Evidence." *The LEGO Foundation*, Nov. 2017, www.legofoundation.com/en/learn-how/knowledge-base/learning-through-play-a-review-of-the-evidence/.

APPENDIX

HOMESCHOOL CURRICULUM

(includes both Christian and Secular Options)

**this is not a comprehensive list, as there are many options from which to choose*

Unschooling

You probably won't find any unschooling curriculum options, because that is kind of the point of unschooling; however, here is a book for parents to look at this method more in depth: *Unschooled* by Kerry McDonald.

Unit Studies

Five in a Row – fiveinarow.com

Gather 'Round Homeschool – gatherroundhomeschool.com

Ivy Kids – ivy-kids.com

Konos – konos.com

Learning Adventures – learning-adventures.org

Little Rabbit Trails – littlerabbittrails.com

My Father's World – mfwbooks.com

Tapestry of Grace – tapestryofgrace.com

Weaver Curriculum – aop.com/curriculum/weaver

Winter Promise – winterpromise.com

Traditional

Abeka – abeka.com

BJU Press – bjupress.com

BookShark – bookshark.com

Calvert Homeschool – calverthomeschool.com

Christian Light – clp.org

LIFEPAC – aop.com/curriculum/shop-lifepac

Oak Meadow – oakmeadow.com

Rod and Staff – rodstaff.com

Switched-On Schoolhouse – aop.com/curriculum/shop-switched-on-schoolhouse

Classical

Classical Conversations – classicalconversations.com

Logos School – logosschool.com

Memoria Press – memoriapress.com

Tapestry of Grace – tapestryofgrace.com

Veritas Press – veritaspress.com

Charlotte Mason

Ambleside Online – amblesideonline.org

An Atmosphere of Learning Bundle – littlehousebecameahome.com

Build Your Library – buildyourlibrary.com

Beautiful Feet Books – bfbooks.com

Blossom & Root – blossomandroot.com

Charlotte Mason Research Company – charlottemason.com

Charlotte Mason's Alveary – charlottemasoninstitute.org

Five in a Row – fiveinarow.com

A Gentle Feast – agentlefeast.com

Master Books – masterbooks.com

Queen Homeschool – queenhomeschool.com

Simply Charlotte Mason – simplycharlottemason.com

Sonlight – sonlight.com

Winter Promise – winterpromise.com

Free

Ambleside Online – amblesideonline.org

Connections Academy – connectionsacademy.com

Discovery K12 – discoveryk12.com

Easy Peasy All-in-One Homeschool – allinonehomeschool.com

Free Homeschool Deals – freehomeschooldeals.com

Homeschool Printables for Free – homeschoolprintablesforfree.com

How to Homeschool for Free – howtohomeschoolforfree.com

Khan Academy – khanacademy.org

Online/Distance Learning

BJU Press Homeschool – bjupresshomeschool.com

Calvert Homeschool – calverthomeschool.com

Connections Academy – connectionsacademy.com

Discovery K12 – discoveryk12.com

Dreaming Spires Home Learning – dreamingspireshomelearning. com

HomeLink Online – homelinkeducation.com

K12 – k12.com

Liberty University Online Academy – liberty.edu/ms/online-academy

Monarch – aop.com/curriculum/shop-monarch

Oak Meadow – oakmeadow.com

Reading Eggs – readingeggs.com

Switched-On Schoolhouse – aop.com/curriculum/shop-switched-on-schoolhouse

Time4Learning – time4learning.com

Specialized Studies

Heritage Studies:

Heritage Mom – heritagemom.com

Brown Sugar & Spice Books & Educational Services, L.L.C. – brownssbooks.com

Woke Homeschooling – wokehomeschooling.com

History:

Curiosity Chronicles – curiositychronicles.org

History Quest – pandiapress.com/history-quest

Math:

Math Mammoth – mathmammoth.com

Math-U-See – mathusee.com

Colosky's Math Academy – coloskysmathacademy.com

Personal Finance:

Dave Ramsey – daveramsey.com/school/homeschool

Reading:

All About Reading – allaboutlearningpress.com

Reading Eggs – readingeggs.com

Progressive Phonics – progressivephonics.com

Science:

Apologia – apologia.com

Classic Science – eequalsmcq.com/ClassicScienceLife.htm

Home Science Tools – homesciencetools.com

The Good and The Beautiful – goodandbeautiful.com

Spelling:

Spelling Power – spellingpower.com

All About Spelling – allaboutlearningpress.com

Typing:

Typing Pal – typingpal.com/en

Legal Services

Homeschooling Legal Defense Association – HSLDA.org/legal

National Home Education Legal Defense – NHELD.com

"HOW TO GET STARTED HOMESCHOOLING" CHECKLIST

- ❑ Pause. Breathe. Reflect. Then proceed.
- ❑ Check your state's legal requirements (and guidelines) at www. hslda.org/legal, www.nheld.com, or www.homeschoolfacts. com to see what you must abide by—this is a starting point, but should not be the final say. If necessary, seek out legal counsel.
- ❑ Locate a local support group—either one in person or on social media, such as Facebook (you can search for homeschooling groups in your geographic area, by religious preference, by homeschooling method, by curriculum choice, etc.)
- ❑ Decide what two to three subjects would you most like your kids to learn. Start with those. Don't try to do every subject to begin.
- ❑ Search for curriculum (free or to purchase), or schedule a consultation to get you started. We would love to assist you during this process.
- ❑ Begin slowly. Keep lessons short and focused.
- ❑ Pick one life skill to work on over the next 12 weeks. Work on it one day a week or once every two weeks. Don't try to do it every day, just try and weave it in as small increments. It could be in the kitchen, laundry, woodworking, auto repair...basically anything that seems of interest to you and your children.
- ❑ Choose one good habit to work developing over the next 12 weeks. Talk about it, and work on slowly building consistency in doing it.

- ❑ Select one thing to do with your hands over the next 12 weeks—possibly a handicraft item. Do that one day a week or once every two weeks. This can add some flavor into your days/weeks.
- ❑ Put together a book basket of beautiful books you would like to read with your kids or want them to pick up and read on their own. Keep it visible. Don't feel tied to it, but use it as an additional option when you want to do something and don't know what to do.
- ❑ Plan to get outside. Enjoy nature. If a day of homeschooling isn't going well, just head out the door and relax. Try again the next day.
- ❑ Be sure to enjoy your kiddos. Appreciate this time together and know that being together is more important than doing all the right stuff with them.
- ❑ Remember this isn't an exhaustive homeschooling list. This is to help get you started while you are figuring things out. Over time, as you become more comfortable and confident in what you are doing, you will become aware of when you need to increase what they are learning.

Let's teach our children to care—about God, people, society, and our country. That isn't done strictly through academics, but through us caring and passing that along to our children. Charlotte Mason said, "The question is not,—how much does the youth know? when he has finished his education—but how much does he care? and about how many orders of things does he care? In fact, how large is the room in which he finds his feet set? and, therefore, how full is the life he has before him?" (*School Education*). We want to be able to say, and hope that our children join along with us, "I Care."

www.ingramcontent.com/pod-product-compliance
Lightning Source LLC
Chambersburg PA
CBHW071311030726

47594CB00002B/386